T0193932

THE LORD AND I

A Face Only the Lord and a Mother Could Ever Love

ALVIN WRIGHT

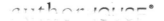

AuthorHouse™
1663 Liberty Drive
Bloomington, IN 47403
www.authorhouse.com
Phone: 1 (800) 839-8640

© 2018 Alvin Wright. All rights reserved.

No part of this book may be reproduced, stored in a retrieval system, or transmitted by any means without the written permission of the author.

Published by AuthorHouse 08/24/2018

ISBN: 978-1-5462-1197-6 (sc)
ISBN: 978-1-5462-1196-9 (e)

Print information available on the last page.

Any people depicted in stock imagery provided by Thinkstock are models, and such images are being used for illustrative purposes only. Certain stock imagery © Thinkstock.

This book is printed on acid-free paper.

Because of the dynamic nature of the Internet, any web addresses or links contained in this book may have changed since publication and may no longer be valid. The views expressed in this work are solely those of the author and do not necessarily reflect the views of the publisher, and the publisher hereby disclaims any responsibility for them.

Everything you read is all true and my own opinion. I was told advice is free. Take it or leave it. This book is for the lost souls out there who need help, and hopefully my story will inspire them. Amen!

IN 1953, VIVIAN JUST FINISHED babysitting for friends she knew in town. The highest grade she completed was the second grade. Her mom had given birth to four boys and four girls. The last one was at eight months pregnant. Her whole life was taking care of children, and when she died, almost two hundred kids visited at her showing. Where she worked at the bowling alley, they put a plaque in her honor in the nursery.

An elderly man made a pact with Pappy. He never had a drink again. In 1954, he never met one in my life named that. I have a face only the Lord and a mother could love, and I'm the greatest family a person could ever have to come into.

It was a hot day, and the town drunk was hanging around. He was a bum and a drunkard. As the old saying goes, he was "Jack of all trades, but master of none." One night he was getting drunk, lurking about and staring at people with his beady eyes. He punched the oldest daughter. Reeking of whiskey breath, he was raping her. She was clawing with every ounce of her strength. She was five foot four and weighed 110 pounds, and she was taking the thrashing of her life. Then it was over. To her dying day, she never touched a drop of alcohol. Then I was created.

If you want to feel sympathy, please don't. I don't believe in it at all. I will tell you about it later. So may the saga, adventure, or journey begin. After that trek began, my mom didn't know what to do so she named me Alvin. In those days of old, as an unwed person, you were considered a society outcast. But luckily a man in her community said he would be my father. His name was Fields. That's how I got my middle name that I have today.

This book tells the story of a boy, a hillbilly actually, who traveled from the rural hills of Kentucky to the state's biggest metropolis. What these eyes have seen and these ears have heard—segregation, assassination, catastrophes, rioting, and so on—will just blow you away.

There are always family secrets, both hard times and good. One brother told me I was perfectly unique. The other one said I was the butcher of the English language.

If you believe in a Lord and Savior, this book is for you. Well then, here is some of the work. Do I have a power inside me? Yes, I do. Everybody does. You just have to know how to use it, as you will soon find out.

A boy was born on June 16 in Ironton, Ohio. No one recalls the year precisely. He had an older brother, William, and two sisters, Marcellus and Olive. In 1927, everybody had to go through a rough depression, standing in lines blocks long and waiting for his or her allotment. In 1927, Pappy used his harmonica to make money by playing songs for people. Some may call it begging, but Pappy always said he was earning his money to eat by singing for others.

In 1928, Forest was soon to be my pappy. He wanted to head out to see the world. No cars were around, so he picked the next best way to travel and hopped on a train to go places. He visited all forty-eight states because that's all there were back then. Given the Depression, his source of income was doing any work he could. He said he would go four to seven days in a week before he found something that paid. He smoked the cigarette and cigar butts he would pick up after people would throw them down. So he traveled until 1932 when a train dick, or someone like that, in Omaha, Nebraska, told him, if he ever saw him again, he would kill him. So Pappy went back to his hometown.

He reminisced about spending the last five years moving from boxcar to boxcar, keeping one eye open all the time. So he finally got back home safely in one piece. Pappy's brother, William, asked if he wanted to go to Detroit for some shindig up there. So of course, they were hot to do that. In 1935, Mamaw gave birth to an auburn-haired girl, Vivian Mae, also called Scratch. She lived up to that title. With her shears, she would give Edward Scissorhands a run for his money. From then on, they gave birth to a child every three years.

In 1938, Mamaw gave birth to a set of twins, ornery Marvin Raye and Margaret Faye. Now Marvin was a trip, all five-foot-four and 120 pounds of him and bragging about it. He had black hair. The guy wasn't afraid of anything. Trust me. He would slice you up, dice, mince, julienne, or whatever he wanted to do. If the "Big, Bad Leroy Brown" song played, I would think of him as the one who was doing it with a couple pieces missing. If that didn't work, he would drop a .38 into your system. His twin Margaret was a sweet, strawberry blonde woman. She had the most wonderful husband, Chester Bloomfield. He had a smile I tried to duplicate.

In 1941, Mamaw gave birth to a daughter, Iantha. She had no middle name. She was the first high school graduate in the family. She married a sailor named for Mays Lick, Kentucky, the orneriest man I had ever met. He was ornerier than Marvin was.

Then hell came to town. Pappy was drafted to go to Germany for World War II. When I was a kid, I asked if he ever did like anybody. He told me he liked just one person, Adolf Hitler.

In 1943, Pappy got to come home. The war was over for him and millions of others. They moved into town in 1943. They would catch a ride for a short distance so he didn't have to walk all the way there. They worked for a couple months and headed back home. They were getting homesick. Well, William was, but not Pappy.

They got in on a Friday, so William said, "Let's go to a barn dance." They were popular back then.

Pappy said he was too tired to go dancing, but he would go to see the ladies. In our family, for some reason, we have dancing blood in our veins. We just love to dance. I've given up dancing because I have a rod in my leg from knee to ankle. Then William was reminiscing about the last six years, hopping from boxcar to boxcar, keeping one eye open all the time to survive in the Depression. He saw some heavyweight title fights and a World Series game. He decided to look for a job up the Ohio River.

In 1933, he started working for a company in Kentucky. That spring, he met a woman, Bertha Shoove. They fell in love and started a family on Cabin Creek near Springdale. He was a redheaded, six-foot-two Irishman, and she was four foot nine or ten, give or take a bit, and weighed about ninety pounds.

Back then, he had to walk six miles to work and six miles back home five days a week. Every so often, a driver going his way might pick him up, but those times were few and far between. Cars were scarce back then. Our family was growing: Bertha, Edna, Lovell, Leslie, our half-brother Edvert, and sister Priscilla, also known as Tallybuster Hords. They lived on the hillside along Cabin Creek. This place was not Jerry West's home. He lived in West Virginia. I don't think it runs in together. I don't know for sure.

In 1944, Mamaw gave birth to a black-haired son named Edward, one of the sweetest men you'd ever want to know. I learned a lot from him about how to fight. He'd say, "Let them throw the first punch. Then light their asses up." He was a real strong puncher.

In 1947, Mamaw gave birth to a son, Charles Douglas. He had black hair. I think he had the highest grades of all the kids.

In 1948, Marvin went to his last day of school because he took his pencil and shanked the teacher. He always told me that, when he died, he hoped they'd put some mattress springs on his feet so he could bounce in hell.

Then in 1950, Mamaw gave birth to a set of twins again, Joel Lee and the other one who died. I remember this because of an event that was about to happen.

In 1953, Mamaw was carrying a girl named Carla Ann, a brown-haired girl who was supposed to be born in September, but in August, that event happened.

In 1954, I was born. I was named Alvin Wright. I was a blond-headed little boy who looked like a guy named Howdy Doody. I never saw him on TV so I couldn't tell you for sure. I do have a picture of me from when I was about six to eight months old. Today this picture hangs in my living room with the picture of Pappy and me. In the left bottom corner is a photo of Pappy when he was over in Germany, standing outside his tent.

They say you don't remember too much when you are young. That's BS. We were all living in a house on Stevens Lane. It was a dirt road back then. There was one house on the right and five on the left. We lived in a two-bedroom house with my grandparents, three aunts, and four uncles. We had no bathroom back then. We had to go to the outhouse.

A traumatic event was about to happen to me. It was winter. I was six months old, and I heard Pappy cry out, "Vivian, you got to do something with this child."

They took me to the hospital where I was born. I had a temperature of 105. They said I had pneumonia. They dunked me in some ice water and submerged me in it. I was crying at the top of my lungs. They had to do this every hour, and I had dreams of that event until I was six or seven.

My mom said, "Let me give him a bath."

The nurse said to her, "No matter who gives him a bath, he is going to cry."

I remember the bright lights, and I figured it would happen again. And it did six months later. The bright lights I saw, come to find out, was my photo being taken.

You just don't forget traumatic events. At least I never have. I even remember the sound of the radio on the top shelf in the living room. We listened to the news, music, and some shows on the radio because we didn't have a TV, not for at least two more years. When I was three, the city was going to put water and sewer pipes on our street, which was just a dirt lane that ran in front of our house. That's right. We were just like the Jeffersons, moving on up to the east side. Then we had a pretty good rain, and it was pouring cats and dogs.

When I woke up, I looked out the backdoor. We had three steps, and the water was up to the last step. Pappy always tilled about a half-acre garden in the backyard and raised vegetables of all kinds. He even grew rhubarb for his pie. I couldn't stand the stuff.

About a month later, Pappy got down to the basics. He was going to put in a bathroom for all of us. Now when Pappy worked, you needed to get out of his way. I watched him like a hawk, studying him sawing, planing wood, and so on. He and Marvin put in everything—tub, sink, toilet, and a gas stove. So now we felt like the Hiltons.

Every morning, Monday through Friday, at five thirty, we heard the teakettle go off. I was a sick little kid just about all the time. So that winter, when I was still three years old, I bumped into the little gas stove with my left hip. The burn left a scar there for the rest of my life.

My oldest aunt, Margaret, was getting ready to marry Chester Bloomfield. He was the nicest man I have ever met. He got drafted into the marines at Lejeune in North Carolina. He was the salt of the earth, something like that.

Pappy always told me that, if you do the job right the first time, you don't have to do it over again. We always remember the traumatic events. And trust me. One was right around the corner. My mom used to babysit for people she knew, especially her best friends' kids. My Uncle Edward came in one night and saw mice on top of our quilts. He said they looked like they were in formation to attack.

Pappy said, "What you don't know won't hurt you."

It seemed weird that some woman in town had her nose bitten off by a rat. And it was gone. I was a little slow about talking and realizing some things. If something got broke, I did it, and I got the spanking until I was about five years old. I always hated it when someone couldn't live up to his or her own mistakes. My Uncle Joel and Carla pointed the finger at me all the time. They always said, "Alvin did it."

That traumatic event is right here around the corner. I learned that you could trade in pop bottles for a penny apiece. My Uncle Joel taught me that, so I thought I would try it one time to get me some baseball cards and especially the bubble gum inside it, like my uncle would do. The store was about two blocks away from the house, so I took five bottles to the grocery store. Then on the side of the house, the sidewalk had about a one and a half- to two-inch lift. My toe hit the ledge. I fell and sliced my finger almost completely off. I screamed like a banshee.

Mamaw came running to see what the heck happened. She almost fainted from the sight.

She got hold of a neighbor to run me down to the clinic to take care of it. At the time, my mom was babysitting at a friend's house. My finger was completely gone. It sliced all the tendons in my finger. We didn't have the technology back then so my finger today has a hunchback in it, and there's no way of fixing it. So I still live with it today. I don't want to hear sympathy at all.

One night lying on the floor, my Uncle Edward got up and stepped on my crippled finger. It just lit me up again. It just made it more unbearable to live.

At that time, Aunt Margaret got married to Chester, who was stationed in North Carolina. The following year, 1958, Aunt Iantha graduated. She was the first one to graduate. She met a man from Mays Lick, Ronnie Emmons, the orneriest man I ever met. He joined the navy in late 1958.

While he was in the service, he met a man, John. Ronnie introduced John to my mom by writing letters to her. So Mom and Iantha went to see them in San Francisco. They fell in love and got married in 1959.

At Christmastime in 1959, Mom and Dad got me a present from Santa, a fire truck pedal car from a Company. I was so big and tall that I could only use it a couple times.

They tried to keep me out of the picture in the living room where the ceremony was taking place, so I wiggled my way to see them kiss for the first time. Someone took a picture of their wedding together. Later that year, Pappy's sister, Marcelous, stopped by to say farewell. She and her husband, Cecil Dooley, were heading west to Ajo, Arizona, next to the Mexican border, to work in the copper mines. Then Mom picked up the stakes and moved to California for a few months. She came back pregnant with my brother Gary Wayne, who was born in June 1960.

It was the annual Germantown Fair. Aunt Iantha was over eight months pregnant, bigger than a saw. Uncle Chester and Ronnie went to the Hooky Cookie show to see naked ladies showing everything you could imagine. Aunt Iantha stood outside the exit door, waiting for him. I was hiding behind my mom. When he came out of there, she was waiting for him with a switch. What happened next was the funniest thing I ever saw at the age of six. She was whipping him with the switch, saying, "I'll give you a show when we get home. I'll undress for you, and I'll show you some nakedness." He was so embarrassed. He was saying, "Quit, Annie!" That was her nickname he had for her.

Two weeks later, my first cousin was born. After Labor Day, it was my time for first grade. I went to school, and I did not like it one bit. The first day, I went for lunch and told my mom that school let out early for me. That was the last time I got to use that excuse.

Now I was at the stage of learning things in life to live by. I had just started the first grade. The teacher was harping about something, two new states on the flag, Hawaii and Alaska. I have a knack of watching people's expressions on their faces and attitudes. She was not happy about it, so I told my mom I didn't like her. She went to the principal's office. Then I was in another classroom across the hallway.

My new teacher was Mrs. Goodwin. She looked very young, and I liked her right from the get-go. In 1960, I don't think there was a thing called kindergarten. It would have really helped me out greatly if I had gone. If I had, maybe I wouldn't have such trouble today with the English language. Today the kids get that head start and preschool, and in my opinion, that's great for them.

One thing I've learned is, if you show me once, it was a pretty good sealed deal. I learn really quickly to grasp things because my mind is hungry for knowledge. At six, I learned a lot from Pappy. One thing was, when food was on the table, you eat, and there's no talking. When he took the first bite, sparks would be flying in the kitchen. Every day we had brown beans and fried potatoes, and occasionally we'd have mashed potatoes and cornbread. And trust me. We ate like kings in my opinion, and I still eat it today, maybe sometimes with a juicy ham hock with it. Maybe once a month, we might splurge and get a roast with all the trimming carrots, taters, and celery. Mamaw could cook with the best of them, especially her famous blackberry cobbler. She said it was all in the cobbler, that is, the breading.

That winter, Mom came back in from California while Dad was shipped off to sea. Christmas came, and they got me a pedal car, which I was way too big for because I was tall for a first-grader but thin. They also got me a fishing tackle of lures.

That spring my Uncle Ronnie caught the biggest buffalo carps I have ever seen. The first one was draped over his shoulder, and its tail fin just barely touched the ground. Next time, the fish's tail drug about a foot on the ground, but in my little dark blue eyes, they were gigantic. I hope you are catching some of these names because I am going to just use their names, that is, for my aunts and uncles.

Then Chester took Dad and me to his dad's house out in country around Kentucky. So his dad told me how to put a worm on a hook because my dad didn't know a thing about fishing. So he told me what a bobber does for you. It wasn't five seconds that a bluegill was on my hook. Then Roy told me a little secret that I was great at keeping for my whole life. Here's some tips for you anglers. You could cut them into chunks or bash their skulls and make it bloody. Then be ready for some action. It really worked. It was like a dinner bell going off.

I almost forgot one of the main things in life. Dad brought me a dog from a place called Kodiak, Alaska. He was half cocker spaniel and husky. His name was Alvin. Yes, like the Chipmunks. So it was off to California again for them. Of course I was left behind again in 1961.

Now it was time to knuckle down for knowledge, which I was just starving for at seven. Mamaw started me cooking in the kitchen. We made meringue, coffee, and a lot of other food. It's what made me into the good chef I am today. And every meal I fix and prepare, I always go full force, from preparing it to eating it.

Like Aretha Franklin's song, I have respect for everybody—race, gender, and you name it. I learned young not to be prejudiced to anyone at all, which is a challenging thing for many people. Today it's sickening, but it's true. We had a black family two houses away. I learned from their dad, Old Man Turner. They had some boys and girls, but one boy, Eddie, had a nickname for me. Well, a couple actually. One was Bugs Bunny because of my big ears. Ronnie sold the old man both buffalo carps for five dollars apiece, which weighed about sixty to eighty pounds apiece.

My teacher, Mrs. Wright, was an elderly woman in her forties, but that's my opinion. Now

Margaret and Iantha got married and started families of their own. All my uncles were still at home. It was Halloween, but I was considered too little to go with them. Carla got to go, and she was just eight months older than I was. I had to stay at bay all the time, but I didn't mind.

Pappy watched wrestling every Saturday, and I would be there right beside him, watching. I never saw him get so riled up while watching it—Dick De Bruiser, The Sheik, Bobo Brazil, Haystack Calhoun, and Johnny Valentine. He was always for the good guys, but for me, I was independent. I was just observing the moves they would make. Marvin and Joel would watch sometimes, but not often. Marvin would be revving up his 1951 Fairlane, and Joel and Carla would go roller skating. And as we know with big families and little kids, the walls always have ears!

Pappy talked to Joel about taking me to the skating rink. Buddy, by the time I left there, I was just pushing off on my right leg, but I didn't fall anymore. I would get the biggest blister on the ball of my right foot. In 1962, I was sick that day, and Mamaw said, "Would you like to play a game of checkers?" And I said yes. It was my very first game. I watched Joel play with friends of his, but it didn't seem to be a hard game. I don't know what they did in the 1910s and 1920s. They lit me a new one. I thought, *Damn, Mamaw.*

After that thrashing I got, I never again lost a checker game. The next game we played, it was a stalemate. She said, "You gonna be good at this." And I was.

Then another day, I was sick. The doctor was still coming to make house calls, so I ran and hid in the pantry, but to no avail. I got poked. The next day, I was feeling better. Mamaw told me that there was a candy bar in the breadbox for me. I walked to the kitchen, hoping it was a Mounds or Almond Joy. It was the best feeling ever. It was just like going to church for the very first time. But when I opened it up, it was gone. Either one of my uncles or Carla ate it.

I didn't know what kind of current events happened, but when I got back to the living room, Mamaw said, "April Fool's!"

I asked, "What's that?"

She told me, and I did not like that at all. I felt burning inside me that I couldn't explain. On the play ground I was the alpha of the second grade. I was extremely dexterous with my hands. I would swing across the bars like a chimp, left over right, left over right, and I always knew where my hands were. One day, Carla brought some of her friends over to play a game, and they reeked at it. I observed like always. I tried it and I was like a buzzsaw at it. I thought no one could beat me in this game, but I will meet my maker later on. Joel is in the boyscouts and he showed me pressure points on the body. Like I say I listen and I listen well, and as we know my pressure points on the body and it works. I can tell you one thing. I've never been fooled again. I don't know what happened after that, but I took it out on boys at school. Mamaw or Marvin had to come and get me after school because of my fighting. He kicked me a couple times in my behind because he had to escort me home.

With school out, Joel and Carla started taking me to a place for recreation. Beachwood Park, which doesn't exist anymore. It's now Beachwood Apartments. Kids at school would cheat in board games, and I'm the kind of person who would not play you again because I can't handle something like that.

School let out for the year. One day I thought I would amble on over to Guy's grocery store two blocks away, but Mamaw was looking for me. When I came out, she switched my bare legs all the way home for two whole blocks. Every step felt like a switch.

Yes, we still had mice problems and roaches in the house. We had to call an Orkin man to slay the roaches. But something happened one day. I saw a rat about a foot long, not including his tail. My uncles chased him with hoes, shovels, and pitchforks. They got him cornered again in the tobacco warehouse in our backyard. Then there's the old saying, "Get a rat trap; he comes out fighting." He leapt about four feet in the air. He was just messing with one of my uncles. He was running away, and suddenly Alvin came out of nowhere. He had a rat in his chompers. It was dead as a doornail.

Then one day Mamaw was getting fed up with my behavior. She said, "Young man, you are going to go to church with Joel and Carla."

The purple-colored church bus came. The driver of the bus was a preacher, Eugene Lawrence. I don't know what came through me when I came on the bus, but it was an indescribable feeling, which had to be the Lord. After that, I was good from then on.

We played some games. I didn't know a thing about a church, but I was soon going to find out about life. I learned that somebody died for me, and I thought that was amazing. I learned good from bad at seven years old. You know the old saying, "Too little, too late."

Then Mom, Dad, and my brother got back from California. Something was different. He had a Packard now, a green Nash Rambler station wagon and uglier than hell. Guess what's next? Yep, it was time to go to California.

Whenever Pappy got a newspaper, you didn't touch it until he read it unless it was the cartoons on Sunday. Joel always got the comics. So, Dad took Pappy, Mamaw, Mom, Gary, and me on a trip to go see William, Pappy's brother, in Cincinnati. When we got there, he lived in a big apartment building, and I couldn't believe my eyes. He had five or six beautiful-looking women living with him, and he was smiling like an opossum on a hot Saturday night. They had undergarments hanging in the bedrooms and bathroom, so this would be the last time I would ever see him.

Later in life, I thought what a life he had or even imagined what a way to go. Later we decided to go to Coney Island in Cincinnati, an amusement park that closed in the 1960s or 1970s to a place now called Kings Island. I was watching a ride. Dad put his shoe up against my behind because I couldn't hear him because of all the screaming. I don't know what it is about my behind, but people like to kick it.

It was off to Cali or bust. First stop was a town called Salem, Illinois, where Iantha and Ronnie lived for just a short while with my firstborn cousin, Yvonne. We stayed about an hour and went to Kansas City, Missouri, where Dad was born, but he called it Independence, where a guy named Truman used to live.

Dad had a sister named Betty. Then there was Fletcher and then Gayle. Dad lost his dad at an early age. Dad was born a few months before the due date. He only weighed almost three pounds. He was in the incubator for almost two months. His mom Bessie was a cotton white-headed woman, but sweet as you could get. Her husband, Bob Buckles, was a barber in town. He had pictures of some players from the KC Athletics back then, like Roger Maris and Dick Green. Of course Maris is famous for his flattop haircut.

Betty had four kids. Vicki Lynn was 99.99 percent Cherokee with ebony dark black hair. There was an extremely beautiful Becky. I don't know for sure if that's short for Rebecca. Then there was Margie and Michael. They ran from seven through two years old. Fletcher was a big fellow. He worked at a donut shop next door to his stepdad's barbershop. Gayle was a cashier at the donut shop as well. We stayed there a couple days, and it was off to California.

Brothers and sisters, let me tell you what. It was a killer two thousand miles from where I was from.

Mom hollered out, "Oh my gosh! Oh my gosh!"

Of course someone was going to look. When I did, I saw two people hanging from billboards with hoods on. Yes, they had been hung. I saw oil rigs from Oklahoma to New Mexico and nothing but flatness. I mean, you could see miles up the roads from New Mexico through to LA. Desert and cactuses were all over everywhere. You saw some mesas, plateaus, and then the Sierra Nevada and the Rockies.

We stopped in Nettles, California. It was about a hundred degrees that day. It was dark when we got into the apartment building. That was when I woke up. What was waiting for me there? If I knew the song by Guns and Roses, I would play "Welcome to the Jungle." Thinking about that haul through Texas, New Mexico, and then Arizona, that was about 1,300 or 1,400 miles of pavement. I played a game I made up because I was good with knowing cars from Mercurys, Pontiacs, and Buicks. I think you got a pretty clever idea. Chevrolets always won, but it was fun. And Dad helped me out on some real old cars from 1930s until now. Then I thought about the Stuckey's pecan rolls stops. I believe there were more of them than Cadillacs.

This was 1962. Then somewhere in the southern part of New Mexico or Arizona, I heard my mom cry out loud, "Oh my gosh! Oh my gosh!"

So of course, I looked to see myself. Two people were hanging from a billboard with a hood over their heads. It was early in the morning. I was thinking it was the Western shows on TV. I thought they must have done something bad. Then my dad told my mom the same thing I thought.

We lived in housing or slums, ghettos, or burrows. It was like a war zone out there, people lying stabbed, shot, or beaten down to a pulp. I learned really fast to keep our doors locked all the time and to not let anyone in. Sirens were going off. It was almost nonstop action where we lived in LA. Watts was uprising, and Hell's Angels were shooting and killing all around us. Our safest place was on the naval base, sleeping in our Rambler.

Mom told me during this time that I was listener. She told me what women liked, and she was right on. I learned that later in life. Now today I give advice to people, and I have the sexiest legs. Mom told me that women seem to still love it today, so it seems.

I learned something really quickly. You lock your door right away in the city. People would break into people's apartments nonstop.

We moved a month later to a subdivision of LA, Long Beach. We moved up above a beauty parlor. With my eight and a quarter hat size and my five-foot-four height, this doctor might be right. I might end up being a ballplayer after all.

Dad's worst scare came when Cuba threatened to launch missiles at us. Dad bought me a bowling game that was about four feet long and racked the pins for you by turning a wheel. I think he mainly bought it for himself because he loved to bowl.

Now Gary, who was just turning two, could name cars like I could, just by their shapes. His knowledge of cars awed me. We got models for cars since we were so young.

Our amusement was going to the turnpike or a beach resort in Long Beach, and sometimes we would travel all around the vicinity of LA. I thought seeing a palm tree was a trip, but it was nothing but trunk for sixty feet high before you saw leaves.

We had a really nice landlord. She didn't bother us at all. We had the same TV networks: ABC, CBS, and NBC. We got to watch a show called *Disney Land*. We got to go there. It put Coney Island in Cincinnati to shame. We got to ride the monorail that went all around the park. So Dad got me a Mickey Mouse wristwatch.

Then reality set in. The school was right across the street from where we lived. One thing about LA, it's warmer than heck out here.

When I was young, Pappy would say, "Listen and learn. That's the only way to do things." And of course he was right. One day, the teacher called on me to read a paragraph. Then when I did, all eyes were on me. What the heck came out of my mouth? Boys and girls were snickering about my Kentuckian accent. They never called on me to read aloud again. If I could find a rock, I would have crawled under it. I could feel piercing eyes all over me. So two months later, guess what? Yep! We went back to my hometown. Amen!

It was time for two thousand more miles of traveling. We got back for the rest of the year and had the meanest teacher in Woodleigh School, Mrs. Kratcher. She taught my uncles and aunts, and she wouldn't spare you the paddle if you goofed up. But I was a good boy. I thought, *You aren't getting this behind.*

Summer was here, so we decided to go to Coney Island. It would be the last time I would get there. Yes, it was two thousand more miles, this time San Diego. Of course there was a pit stop at Kansas City, Missouri. We lived in a subdivision called National City. You got it, the war zone. But the apartments were improving each time. Kids were fighting on the playground. Of course you got your bullies, nerds, obese, artistic leaning, slow learning, and, last but the worst person on earth, a Kentuckian. Of course that would be me.

When we had PE, everybody would get picked but me. I was thinking I had leprosy or something. They were calling me nasty names you could not even imagine for a nine-year-old from the sticks of Kentucky. I was glad the artistic got picked because I don't think they had ever been chosen before, so it made me smile to see them grin. It was priceless.

So like I said, you got your groups. The artistic kids opened the door for me to come in. Then there was the nerds and finally the obese. The bullies, thugs, or whatever you wanted to call them, I stayed away from them.

A kid named Billy lived in the complexes like me, but we were in different grades. He was two years older than I was. We were playing around. He got on top of me and wouldn't let go of me, so I remembered the wrestlers Pappy and I used to watch. Then bam! It was over.

He asked, "How did you do that?"

I said my Uncle Joel taught me some good moves, and buddy, do they ever work. They're very efficient. We went to the library and looked in the dictionary, and I saw a picture of the word that scared everybody, "erosion." I also saw a picture on a flag in the library that day. It read, "Don't tread on me."

One day, a thug was picking on an artistic kid, just mauling him for no reason at all. Then something popped. I was like Popeye, "I can't stands no more." After three blows, it was all over but the shouting. All eyes were watching me, and I mean everybody—teachers and bullies. After that, I had at least three fights a week waiting for me. I am not a braggart, but I kicked the bully's tails. I invented the Alvin slouch. I would lay up against the school building with one foot against the wall so I could jump and let anyone who messed with me have it.

Then came the big day, classroom portrait time. I sat in the back of the classroom so I could keep an eye on everybody. I tell you one thing. There was fear in my eyes and heart, but I still got the classroom portrait. The Lord guided every block and punch I did. I love music still today. Out here in California, it was the Beach Boys' song, "Sloop John B."

I kept saying, "I want to go back home."

We took one of Dad's friends to Vegas to pick up his car in the navy. When we got there, the city limits were barren and sandy, and there were no homes. It seemed like a mile or something, so when we left, I looked back at night, and it looked like a bunch of 49ers had camped out there.

Before we moved from San Diego, there was a new punch for me, actually a sucker punch. I can count them on both of my hands, but that was it because I was in lockdown mode. I was bringing the kitchen sink and everything else. I get into it now because it's personal.

Dad took me bowling the first time. If I bowled a fifty, I got another game. I bowled a forty-nine.

It was time to load up the U-Haul trailer. Thank goodness because I thought I was going to die!

One day, the runt of the bullies was talking to me. He seemed to be all right.

"Wrong," one of the nerds said. "Watch your back, Alvin."

Of course he was right. He sucker-punched me and bust my lower lip, but that was his last lick on me. Ding! It was over. After the altercation, some fifth- or sixth-grade girls said, "I found someone to beat you up."

I said and thought to myself, *I'm gonna die here in LA.*

In my neighborhood, I ran to the house, but I decided enough was enough.

One day an adult asked me, "How come you're not running?"

I said, "I'm sick and tired of running."

He laughed out loud and asked, "Where are you from?"

I told him. Then he gave me a tip, to keep my mouth shut.

Guess what? You're right. It was time for two thousand more miles of driving, still playing the most cars for the trip.

We stopped by Kansas City again. I got to see my friend Vicky Lynn and she was the sweetest person that I ever had to talk to. Plus she was the only one to ever talk to me, talk, and talk and talk, but it was music to my ears because for some reason everyone else didn't want to talk to me. So any man who ever married her would be the luckiest man in the world. Dad, Gary, and I all went to see a movie called *It's a Mad, Mad, Mad World*, a comedy. I needed that, but on the way to the house, in the new 1963 Bel Air, the radio broadcast the shooting in Dallas. Dad, a sailor like JFK, took it hard. His jaw dropped really low.

Now I was back in my hometown again. My new teacher, Mrs. Main, thought I had a brain problem, so I went to see a psychologist. I passed with flying colors. Pappy bought a bunch of encyclopedias and medical books, and it was awesome. The pictures were great. I feel like I'm missing something. What it is, I don't know, but maybe I'll figure it out.

Dad gave Pappy a nickname, Tiger, like the Exxon cat back then. Mamaw had plumbing problems, female problems actually. At four foot ten, she went from 90 to 190 pounds. Dad called her Big Bertha, like the play gun back in that era. Let me tell you. She did not like it, and that was the end of that name.

Oh, heck. I felt something in the air. Dad had been here too long. Good call! Two thousand more miles was waiting for my tush. Of course, there was a pit stop in Kansas City and on to Los Angeles again. This time, it was called Bell, California. I heard the mayor had his fingers in the cookie jar for millions of dollars. I saw one hanging from a billboard with a cloth covering his head. Yes, he had been publicly hung from a billboard in southern Arizona.

Welcome to the jungle again. It was a really nice apartment this time with a big swimming pool for renters. We had an uncle and aunt there, along with their son.

Charley and Laura were there with their son Harvey. He had every Justice League of America comic book. He had Superman's first book and all the others' first books but not one Marvel comic book.

Charley's belief was, "Why take down a Christmas tree when you got to put it back up again?" It was the years of *Gilligan's Island* and *I Dream of Jeannie*. It would be our first Christmas away from our hometown. I was still thinking how Dad drove last year from San Diego to LA every day with another crewman. How I missed an extra TV channel. It was in Tijuana, Mexico, just across the border from San Diego.

Every two weeks, I got a buzzed navy haircut. Dad would go to Tijuana to get his hair cut for a nickel because he couldn't cut his own hair. Then Dad bought me a few monster models: Werewolf, Dracula, Mummy, Frankenstein Creature from the Black Lagoon, King Kong, Godzilla, and finally Phantom of the Opera. Our next-door neighbor's son raced go-karts in California a lot, and his would do up to ninety on a straightaway. Dad took a picture of me sitting in it. *Cool*, I thought.

So it was back to reality now. I was watching a movie on TV. I saw it about two or three years ago. Dad saw it on the ship. It's called *Your Cheating Heart*. Chester, Margaret, Mom, Gary, and I went to see it at a drive-in theater. It was a pretty good movie. I couldn't get over how much room there was in Chester's Lincoln International. It was a 1950's model. It was like a motel bed. It was so huge.

But let's go back to the movie. I got a line from it, and I will say it until my dying day, "If the good Lord's willing and the creek don't rise." So here I was, getting ridiculed more than ever, saying things like "You're a freak." Or they'd call me ugly, retarded, or ignorant. On and on it went. The girls were just as bad as the guys were. They wouldn't let me play anything at recess. The town had a recreation park to play, but the price to play was fighting warriors, or so they called it.

Dad bought me a Duncan yo-yo to amuse me, but that didn't last long. Someone took it from me, so it was like it was in San Diego. I can't stands no more. Dad brought another one of his shipmates home for the weekend. He went with me to the amusement park for kids. I thought there wouldn't be any types of conflicts because he was there with me. Boy was I wrong. His name was Midget!

Midget didn't see the initiator who hit me, but he saw me, the retaliator. Midget was a gymnast but had no legs at all. But from the waist up, he was all muscles. His favorite piece of equipment was the rings that hung from the rafters. I also found a new punch—hit and then run! They were faster than I was, thanks to my darn flat feet. It was my first Christmas away from my hometown. I missed those two pieces of chocolate candy that we got every year.

One day the Lord and I made a pact that, if I made it to fifty years old, I would be the happiest man alive. One day the Lord put me in my place. I got cocky and lunged. I ended up with a shiner out of it.

First Mom asked, "What happened?"

"I ran into the side of the classroom door," I replied.

I never ever lunged again in a good fight. Dad was off the next day and took me to school. He told me about Kansas City. He told me he had to fight on the way to and from school every day of his life. Then he said, "I think there is an old saying in the service. If you want sympathy, look in the dictionary. You'll find it between the words 'shit' and 'syphilis,' and you'll find it."

I can't express enough from the abyss of my heart. Folks in small and medium towns and country, you should feel so grateful that you live in those places because, in the metropolis, it's a living nightmare. I just went to elementary school there, and I just cannot imagine what high school would be like.

So I busted a few skulls then, it seems. It was like hundreds of kids were watching this.

Then I yelled out, "If you want a piece of this freak, come and get it."

Damn, about fifteen to twenty kids were coming over.

Then I said, "Wait in line, and you get your chance. But it has to be one at a time."

And they did.

One thing I had going for me was that I was tall. I was ten and over five foot tall, so I figured I would jab like Joel taught me and Edward, saying "Let them come." And people, it works. I went about two or three times a week or less, sometimes zero. I would have a line of fifteen kids waiting for me. Like I said, "One at a time." The most I fought in one day was nine kids.

It was around Thanksgiving that I made a vow with God. If I made it to fifty, I would be the happiest man in the world. This came from a ten-year-old.

It was Christmas break when I noticed that there was nobody around to fight me. I thought it was the end of time or something. Then some pretty girl in my class played a game with me. It was about a ten- to fifteen-foot wall, and we had to hit with the ball of our fist. Then we had to let it bounce before we could hit it. Of course, with my accent, I was going to whip her, and she thought I was going to spank her.

School started again, and they had a new name for me, Lurch. That's right, the guy from *The Addams Family*. They had something like a witch's hat shape with rings to swing around the hat, and I flew around it with great ease. I had to bend my knees because I was so tall, so that was how I got the name Lurch. But the best part of it all was I got so much respect from all the kids, boys and girls. And I was getting good in accents now.

You got it. It was time for two thousand more miles. First, we stopped at a place called Ajo, Arizona, where Marcelous lived. Before we got there, we stopped at San Bernardino for gas. Mom carried Gary to the bathroom, so he left without any shoes on. The concrete was smoking. His feet blistered badly. I laughed so hard that I was crying. But Gary had a short temper. I know it's wrong to laugh about stuff like that, but if I had video camera, you all would laugh hard too.

We had to go right, turning at Gila Bend, to get to Ajo, right next to the Mexico border. It would be the last time I would see the Dooleys. Every time we went west, we stopped by for a visit. Of course, Kansas City was next for the next 1,400 miles. Like Johnny Cash, my all-time favorite singer, sang, "I've been everywhere."

Iantha and Ronnie were expecting a child again, Penny Jo. They lived in Lexington, Kentucky. Now if you say you are a true blue UK fan, Ronnie pumped blue all the time. I knew until he died that he kept score sheets on every player and MVP for that game. He got me liking basketball. He took me out to shoot, but only thing I was good at was free throws. And 90 percent the way I shot it, it was called the granny shot, underhanded. Only person I ever see shoot it like that was a guy named Rick Barry with a 90 percent lifetime.

So yes, it was another school, Deep Springs Elementary. Penny Jo was born, and Ronnie said he would never be broke because he had a Penny.

You got it. Another current event was about to happen to me. Penny was five or six days old when I held her, and I was playing with her. And when Iantha changed her, her cord was bleeding. It scared the crap out of me, so from that day on, I never held a baby with the cord still attached, not even my own kids.

It was back to my old stomping grounds again for two months at Woodleigh. One day some kids were picking on some boy named Leroy, a heavyset black kid. Some boys wanted me to kick his ass, but these kids were prejudiced as all get off, so we traded a few blows. Then I thought, *This kid hasn't done anything to me.* So I quit because I felt like I was being a bully.

One day in the future, I saw him, and he asked, "You want to finish that fight back then?"

So I just walked away, so Leroy, I am sorry about what happened.

Well, I guess you know it's that time again. You betcha. This time it was Zion, Illinois, on Gabriel Street. We had to put a bullet in the Nash Rambler for a Chevy II Nova station wagon, yellow at that. There was no more sunny weather now. Let's have some snow days instead and blistering winds off from Lake Michigan. Oh yeah!

Dad asked, "Do you want to make some money?"

I said yeah, so I went door to door selling *TV Guides*. I had good sales at the time and made some good money.

So now it was beginning to start the comic book era and baseball cards. When we moved in, the landlord came and ask if Mom ironed clothes. Mom said yes, and this pretty decent-sized man was talking about a man who wrestled a bear, Paul "Bear" Bryant. He coached the Alabama team, and while rambling, some quarterback got drunk with a bunch of pretty women. Pappy told about a man wrestling a bear. I thought it was fiction. So that was my college team on football, along with Notre Dame gold and green attire. In Chicago, they showed a lot of Notre Dame.

I remember one game for number one and two against Michigan. It was a tie, 10-10. Also I remember their school music for Notre Dame. I started shooting and playing basketball, and I was getting good. I shot a free throw, and if I made it, it was an easy layup by using the backboard of course. But if I missed, I had to shoot it where it landed. My favorite spot on the court was the base line. So call the fire department because the nylons were smoking hot. I'm going to take advice from San Diego, to keep my mouth shut.

One thing I loved right away was the WGN network. It was awesome. The only baseball team I really knew were the Cincinnati Reds. Now there were two teams up here, the Cubs and White Sox, on WGN. The school was all right. There were no problems for a month and a half.

Then the head student asked me, "Who do you pick in the World Series, Dodgers or Twins?"

I never heard of any of them, so I said Dodgers. Then I got a sneering look from him when I spoke. So far, there were no problems clear up to about spring. I found my favorite sport, hockey, specifically the Chicago Blackhawks.

In the spring, some bully kept picking on this little kid, and I mean mauling him good outside while we were waiting for the school doors to open. He was in the other sixth grade.

I yelled out, "Quit picking on him!"

So he came over and got in my face. "What are you going to do about it?"

I said, "Just leave him alone. He wasn't doing anything to you."

He swung and missed me. I jabbed him in the face. Then it was on, blow for blow, toe to toe. Then kids got in between us, and it was over. The kid never picked on him again. But I learned a valuable thing that day. I never took up for anyone again because it wasn't worth it. I valued life more than that.

Then the Cubs hit the field, and I fell in love with them and Jack Brickhouse, the announcer. I discovered something while watching the ballgame, specifically the Pirates versus the Cubs. I remember it like it was yesterday. I was seeing auras on people, that is, for goodness and death.

I asked Mom, "Do you see this white around this guy's head?"

"No," she said.

So the Lord must have given me a gift of seeing goodness and death. Remember this stuff because it occurs a lot in the future. The first person I saw was one of the greatest to play, Roberto Clemente. He moved with so much gracefulness. He run, hit, and fielded like no one I have ever seen. When the Lord made him, he broke the mold, so people missed out on seeing him play. He was the greatest player I ever saw, in my opinion. Amen.

And the first time I saw *Rudolph the Red-Nosed Reindeer*, I knew what it felt like being a misfit, not wanted, not having people anything to do with you. I was like the obese and any other people who are made fun of on a daily basis. I was always the misfit, just like poor old Rudolph.

That spring still, eleven dads said, "I got a job for you if you want it, selling *TV Guides* to people around town."

I didn't know how long *TV Guides* had been out, so I said I would. I took to it like a champ, selling them left and right. Oh, how the money rolled in. I had a King Kong piggy bank. It was over half full of money. I bought every baseball card from the 1964 through 1968 seasons. Yeah, I got the Pete Rose Rookie of the Year card to Nolan Ryan's mug, and I got two of them.

In 1963, Joel was playing some football. In the lane, he was the Cowboys. I was the Packers. So the Packers won the first Super Bowl and then again the next year. I am a Chicago sports fan in everything except football. Green Bay is my team. I thought the big G on their helmet meant "God" to me.

Then that year, Chicago got another team, the Bulls, and I fell in love with them right away. The Packers beating the Cowboys in Dallas was an explosive game to the very end. Then they wiped the floor with the Chiefs.

My team hit the court for the first time ever. After the Chicago Bulls' very first game, I was a huge fan ever since. Any Chicago sport is my team, except for Green Bay in football.

I ran into the bully and his thugs again while I was practicing free throws, and I thought this was the end because he had two friends with him. But luckily they just walked on. Praise the Lord. I passed the sixth grade with thirty-six grades, and thirty-two were Fs. Gym was the only one I passed. So I was placed in the seventh grade. I learned the languages a lot better and passed with flying colors. Dad, cruel after all them Fs, called me something like Dino the Dinosaur.

Now Dad didn't allow us to watch *Batman* or *Star Trek* at home. He thought it was malarkey.

Edward got married now, and so did Marvin. Charles got drafted in the navy and got boot camp in Great Lakes. He came home to us when it was over and stayed with us until he got stationed somewhere. He bought a *Playboy* magazine. It had a set of identical twins for a centerfold.

I thought I'd try buying friendship in the seventh, but it did not work out at all. The first guy went three weeks, and not one word was said to me. I skipped him for another person, and in three weeks, there was nothing. PE rolled around, and the first guy got cocky. I blasted his jaw. I went to my locker, and out of nowhere came the biggest sucker punch I ever had. Someone hit me dead in the belly, and I gasped and gasped. Before I got my wind back, he apologized at least ten times. I don't know if the Lord made him say he was sorry or if someone in the locker room didn't like it, but the apology came from somewhere.

Oh, yeah, it was time to move again. In 1967, it was back to Lexington, Kentucky. Again at least it was my home state. Bryan Station Junior High was where I went. There were no problems at all. There of course was bullying, but I just ignored it. When I told you in 1962 that I would meet my maker I did in 1967, I met them while I was playing a game. It was Iantha, she asked me what I was doing? I replied playing a game of jacks. She said "I'll play you a game. I went first, went through 3 sets and then she went through 7 sets before she missed. Then I missed in the next two sets, then she wiped me clean and asked me if I wanted to play again? I said sure. I went first and went through four sets before I missed, and then she went and went ten sets straight, I had never seen that done before. I call that an ass whopping by my Auntie!!But no one has ever beat me at a game of jacks after Iantha, and she said to me, that I was the ONLY boy who she had ever seen play that game. I would buy the one inch metal jacks and I had them embedded prints in my palms, fingers, and sometimes cuts especially if you play on concrete. To me the hardest thing about jacks was the split jacks, and that's when the ball hits the jacks and caroms off, I caught about 40% of the time and you have to say split jacks when it happens. Caution sometimes when this happens the jack can fly anywhere, it can hit you in the face, in the eye, and etc, so be careful it hurts!

When I was a kid, I read Pappy paper cartoons and sports. I saw a weird team called UCLA. That was what I thought it spelled. I found out this year what it meant, and I was living in LA. Ronnie, like I said, bled blue, but the year before, Kentucky lost to West Texas State. I was shocked. Dad watched it. Yeah, I'm a UCLA rooter all the way.

I passed school with flying colors again.

But one day, some girl behind me said to me, "You're smart."

Elizabeth was her name, and she was only the first girl in my life who smiled at me and the first person to ever talk to me. I'm the most gullible thing that every walked. I was naïve. I didn't know why someone would have to lie.

I was getting some baseball cards when Ronnie asked me to ask the clerk if she had any mating all.

She gave me a stare off the chain. "I think you better go, son."

When we were living in Chicago, we had several chilly days. One day it was forty below, not including wind chill.

I would read the neighbor's newspaper, the *Chicago Tribune*. I would see something called the Dow Jones, and I saw one that stuck in my head, IBM. So I asked dad what he thought.

He said, "Don't waste your money on it."

I probably should have asked Ronnie instead.

In my opinion, I saw the greatest basketball player ever. It was Lew Alcindor back then. Now it's Jabbar. Ronnie was a Big E fan from Houston. Elvin Hayes was being named, and they played in the Astrodome. They lost, but Lew Alcindor had a scratched eyeball and had to wear goggles so I lost a bet to Ronnie for a meal on the town. It was the only college game the man ever lost.

So Dad worked with Ronnie at Standard Products in Lexington. He also took a part-time job as a naval recruiter for servicemen.

One day we went with him, and Mom said, "Look how your daddy can talk with his hands."

I never noticed it. So about two months later, you got it. It was time to move again, this time to Lynchburg, Virginia. He reenlisted into the navy. He had begun recruiting after sixteen years in, so he began to be a recruiter.

A guy named Milberg averaged about forty-five points a game. He got sixty-five against UK, but they still lost. I think he scored over four thousand points in three years, and there was no three-point shot back then. Or he would have probably scored six thousand points in his three years.

Then in 1967, the SEC conference had its first African American at Vanderbilt. He was named Wallace, but he was good. I was so proud of the SEC, and other conferences started doing the same. And I said, "Amen!"

Then I saw a man named McClain pitch a thirty-game winner. And he was darn good. He won something called the Red Rooster Award a few times as a naval recruiter. Now was the time for a guy named Pistol Pete Mara Vick with his floppy socks.

So what happened? Martin Luther King Jr. and Robert Kennedy were slain for no reason at all. So like I said, if I make it to fifty, I'll be the happiest person alive.

While getting ready for high school, Dad taught me two things so far. In the fifth grade, he taught me, if you want sympathy, go look in the dictionary between "shit" and "syphilis." You will find it. I think it was some navy expression. Next, he taught me you won't be able to count all your loyal friends on both hands for the rest of your life, and he was so right.

When I came in with a busted lip or a shiner, that was what he told me about sympathy. In Kansas City, he fought from start of school to the end of the day. Folks, that's just the life in big cities.

I started out in a school called Link Home. The first time to the bathroom, it was like AC/DC's song, "Dirty Deeds." It was time for the high school head to come a calling. We sized each other up. Then he offered me a cigarette. I said I didn't smoke, and it was over.

Two months later, you got it. It was another school across town called Sandusky. It was the same thing. The high school head confronted me, and it was over with no problems at all.

Everything was just going on great. I was wrestling at school in gym and still undefeated. One day in biology, some student showed me someone wrote "Alvin Wright and Amanda." I never met her, but it lightened my heart. I saw her two years later in the yearbook, and her beauty amazed me.

Nineteen sixty-nine, oh what was lying ahead for me. One student went undefeated. He was about two hundred-some pounds, and I was a mere one hundred and forty. He smarted off to me, and I kicked him where the sun didn't shine.

He turned around, and I was about to pounce on him. And he said, "I don't want to fight."

But he would wrestle me, and it would be the last day of school. Mr. Gregory, the biology teacher, was the referee, and I tell you what. That whole gym was packed. No one really cared about the kid, and they were all rooting for me to win. I didn't know how to feel.

At the beginning of the year, my wrestling idols were the Minnesota Wrecking Crew. It was elbows, knees, lifts, and firemen carries. I brought the kitchen sink, but so did he. We wrestled outside the mat, throwing forearm shivers. Mr. Gregory tried to get us back on the mat. Everything was a big blur to me. I think Amanda was the biggest cheerer of all. Like I said, it was all a blur. I went for the pin on him, but the ref grabbed my hands, holding onto the mat, so I tried the Sheik's famous move, the camel clutch. But it fell so I tried the claw move on his temple. All he did was squeal like a madman.

About thirty minutes into the match, people were roaring. The worst thing happened. He got me in the scissors around my waist and squeezed the air out of me, and it was over. No punches were thrown because it would have been all over then in wrestling. It was the last class of the day with about fifteen minutes to go. No one said one word.

I know one thing for sure. I miss *Jeopardy* with Art Fleming up in the Chicago region and *Dark Shadows*. Maybe in Virginia I will get to see them again.

Someone was wanting to know if I would go up to a place called Woodstock. I was just fourteen, and she was still fourteen. She was a wild one now. She drank like a fish and took drugs. She made up for all her brothers and sisters and their good behavior. One song summed her up, "White Rabbit."

They shot a rocket into space and landed on the moon, so they say, and televised it on all network stations. I was doing paper delivery, mowing yards, and raking in the cash. I'd be starting my first real paying job at a McDonald's. I was a Big Mac flipper, and they just really came out with them.

But before that happened, you know there's a storm brewing for the next day. And baby, I wasn't lying. For some reason, there was that, and a hurricane was brewing off the coast of Norfolk, Camille. Brother, she was nasty. We lived two hundred miles from the coast, and all low-lying areas were washed away. Homes were gone. People were floating down the creeks on coffee tables to survive. It was devastating. Dad had to go around and rescue people all around the low-lying areas. He said it was awful and sickening.

I think I heard a news station say it blew a baby whale up the James River next to Richmond. It had winds up to 190 miles an hour. I wish they had the Weather Channel back then for coverage. It was sickening, I tell y'all. To me, Katrina was bad, but not as bad as Camille was.

We went to Pappy's home for our annual Labor Day get-together, and Carla gave me a piece of paper and told me to take it when I felt like it.

School started, and it was the first year for segregation. And let me tell you. It was not pretty. In cities that big, you got your gangs all over town, just waiting for a riot. I was sitting in English class one day and remembered that someone gave me a piece of paper. What did she call it? Blotter acid?

I'd never done anything like that before, so after a half hour had gone by, something was going wrong between my ears. I looked at the clock on the wall, and the hour hand was circling around really fast. My heart started pounding away. I think we had about five more minutes left, but it seemed like two hours. I was hoping no one would call on me.

The bell finally rang, and buddy, I ran down the hall about a hundred feet to the exit door. So I ran, and it seemed to take five minutes to get students hollering at me, "Where are you going?"

I thought to myself, *I am heading home.*

I got on the city bus and just closed my eyes. I got home and told mom I didn't feel well. I had to come home and get well. I shut the door and didn't come out until supper. When I was in there, I discovered some amazing things in my brain. This drug is *not* for everyone. If you're paranoid, then stay away. My drug was acid. I saw so many colors. It was so psychedelic. It was my favorite of all. It was like an explosion in my head with amazement, but you shouldn't do liquor with it.

But whenever I could, I would take any acid. There is the good, the bad, and so on, just for that good feeling. Gary had an anger problem during this time, and this drug and I saved Gary from a lot of trouble during that time.

One day I started smoking cigarettes, Chesterfield, which they don't make anymore. After two packs, I found out why they went out. So now it was Winston with its full flavor.

One day I got up and looked in the mirror, and I was horrified to see a face like mine. I think it was because I had been told so much how ugly I was and called stupid. You know, after a while, it will get to a person. So I concluded what I was. I didn't know it at the time, but I was a rogue. I didn't want nobody around me or be around them.

Now I was thinking, *What could be waiting around the corner for me?* I was getting ready to find out. One day at work, I heard some people talking about going to a concert, so one day a guy and girl asked if I wanted to go and see Iron Butterfly play. I said sure. I had saved up to about $1,000 in my time, and I was a going to have a fun time. I told Mom I was staying over at a worker's house for the night. I tell you this. I never lied to anyone but to my mom all my life because she was a worrywart, so we called it in my time.

I said, "Well, sure." We got to the concert, and we stayed together until it started. Then we split up. When the concert started, someone passed a cigarette, or so I thought. But it was Mary Jane (marijuana). I laughed so hard when we got back to the car. I couldn't hardly stop laughing.

Here mom (Vivian) was about to pop little brother into life. Gregory Douglas, like Charles's middle name, was born on October 20. It was the first day we had chilly weather. Still today he loves the cold, and I don't.

When we lived in Chicago, one weekend I was playing on the schoolyard with a 180-pound Saint Bernard. You picked up the ball; you would get knocked down with all 180 pounds. I had the best time of my life then, but of course, something always came with it. We played about two hours more. It was cold, and I came in.

Mom was howling at me, saying it was time to come in right now, like she did previously. I yelled back that I was having too much fun. I came in then. I noticed my fingers and toes were still numb. Fingers first got back feeling. My toes were thawed two days later, and still today, if I'm out in the cold too long, they start hurting again. My fingers aren't as bad, but on some days when it gets about forty to sixty degrees, they told me it feels like ice cubes. And let me tell you, it turns off a woman. I always thought it was frostbite, but I'm not a doctor. Remember this date because it will pop up again and again. Get my drift?

It would also be my last time to go out on Halloween because Gary and the boy next door went out to trick-or-treat. The kid had some M80 firecrackers. And let me tell you something. They got a powerful punch to them because in Lexington I blew up some neighbor's trash can. I mean the lid flew off the can. The kid would drop one in someone's pumpkin if we didn't get any candy.

We journeyed quite a bit. We blew up a pumpkin, but the third one was completely different. The people didn't answer the door. The pumpkin blew, and some guy came out with a pump rifle. We ran then. He must have shot into the air because he could have had Gary. We ran into the back then. We ran into a briar patch or thickets, whatever you call it. The thrones cut like a knife. I lost my hard sole shoes in there, and I wasn't about to go back after this traumatic event.

Went to the bowling alley with dad and mom. Went to the plaza. I only had two dollars to my name and I went to the department store and checked out the 45 records. I had enough for only one record. But Carla I seen put six to ten 45 records in her waist, and didn't get caught. I bought one and I decided to steal another one. I went back into the store to steal it, after getting it, as I was leaving the store a cop said "what do you have in the bag?" "BUSTED!! I said thank you Lord, because I never, ever stole again. The 45 I stole, was "Daddy sings base", by Johnny Cash.

The Milwaukee Bucks, who had the worst record in the NBA, got Jabbar. I think they had the second-best record to the Lakers, 69-13, which stood for many years. The fall next year, they got my second all-time favorite player on my team, Oscar Robertson (Big O). If anybody needed to get respect, it was him. He started with the Royals. He had Jerry Lucas, who also won an NBA title on different teams. Also now I turned the big sixteen.

Now I am going back to some of the wild days, a blast from the past. For entertainment, we had a radio in the living room on a shelf in there. The TV came about 1957. A person parked his car across the lane with a big car garage with a large bunch of poison ivy. So my Uncle Joel said one day that, if you eat a poison ivy leaf, you never catch it again. Yes, gullible me tried it. I caught it in my throat and had to get a shot and some medicine with it, but you know, whatever was in it, today I can't catch it. People, there's one thing about me. I don't BS at all.

Then there was a Mercury, a black and yellow one. I was in the backseat, and there was a gigantic spider around my neck and shoulder. It was huge, and Mom said, "You really remember that event." Something like that you don't forget, at least I don't.

Then again in 1961, the next-door neighbors had a person drop by and holler at them. And everybody knows that everybody's good. He was heading to Cincinnati, so I asked if I could come with him.

He said, "Go ask your mama."

I came back out and said it would be all right, but I didn't ask at all. I got back about five hours later. I told her everything, but it wasn't about what was going to happen.

She led into me with a willow switch, and believe me, they wrapped around the legs good, especially when they were bare legs. It was the worst whipping I ever had in my whole life, and I had my share.

She asked me, "Are you going to ever do it again?"

I said, "No, I wouldn't, Mom."

But she kept giving it to me. Then I made a mistake and said yes.

Then she asked "What?" and wailed a lot more so I didn't know what to say.

After about four to five minutes of thrashing, she quit. I had welts around all my legs, but I never did it again.

Now the poison ivy event, I don't recommend it, but like I said, I can't catch it anymore. Poison oak? Hell, yes, I can. I had every pox. You name it, I probably had it. I did not like the smallpox shot because I had to wear a plastic shield over it from getting bumped and had to take it twice in first and fifth grade.

In San Diego in 1962, the next-door neighbors were watching *I Dream of Jeannie* and *The Beverly Hillbillies*. That show reminded me of us from the South. Dad didn't like it at all until he saw an episode about Jethro, and he almost bust a gut. In my opinion, he was greener than a gore. I always liked Granny because she reminded me of my Mamaw, all four foot ten and 90 pounds of her. Then my dad bought some country music, and he let me buy one. It was *Meet the Beatles*, their very first album. I cherished it.

The Wizard of Oz came on every fall, and Pappy was always getting a box of Russell Stover's candy, the two-layered one, and we all got three pieces apiece. We all took our turn. The Company gave him one every year before Christmas.

I tell you right now. I am not a TV person at all because I think it was all the soap operas that my mom would watch. Myself, it was sports, sports, and a whole lot more and, of course, *Jeopardy* and *The Beverly Hillbillies*. Dad and Mom liked the *Andy Griffith Show*, and really the only show I liked that they did was *Dragnet* when Joe Friday would say, "Just the facts." I still say that today. I also liked the *Carol Burnett Show*.

Going to Bell, California, we saw another hooded person hanging from the billboard. The Greyhound was doing about eighty to ninety. The speed trains were hollering about seventy to eighty speeds in the southern parts of New Mexico and Arizona.

Then we remembered the slaying right down the road—a hop, skip, and a jump. The man's name was Richard Speck. He went berserk, killing eight nurses. It would have been nine, but she hid under the bed, probably praying for dear life. I bet she still has nightmares today. I know I would.

Out West, I saw kids get slugged by their dads, and I mean fists, not slaps. They came in black and blue. On one occasion we were changing in gym, and the boy had an iron burn mark on his back. I don't know if it were an accident or not, but I felt truly graceful where I was at.

But the worst thing that hurt me was when the Reds traded Frank Robinson. He was headed to the Orioles, so right there I was a Cubs fan from then on. Robinson won the Triple

Crown in his first year at Baltimore. The greatest fun I ever had was when a boy had a Saint Bernard. If you picked up the football, he would knock you down. We would play for hours. I ended up with ten frostbitten toes, along with ten frostbitten fingers.

I watched Captain Kangaroo in the morning and Diver Dan, and in the Cincinnati area, we had a show called *Uncle Al Show with Wendy*. Then in the mid and late 1960s, there was *American Bandstand*, where the action was, and of course *The Monkees*. But in Chicago, we got the *Bozo Big Top*. I went to the Kentucky State Fair in Lexington and saw Bonnie and Clyde's automobile. And let me tell you. That thing was full of bullet holes on both sides. Then Mom won a trip to some place, and the people next to us won a drawing.

Let me tell you again that I don't go looking for trouble. It sometimes always finds me. Gary was always getting into kids bigger than he was, and I had to finish them off. It was someone my age or in between our years. Because I quit running in San Diego, that was the last time for that.

Charles got married, and Joel wasn't too far behind him. But Joel got drafted so Dad recruited him. He got sent off to a place called Iceland, but when he was there, he got to see Led Zeppelin doing album three. The Led Zeppelin song was the "Immigrant Song" because they were about to leave when a major snowstorm struck and they had to stay there for a week.

One of the good times I remember was in Chicago. They sold Coca-Cola bottle caps with a football on the lid, Bears on one side and all stars on the right, but if you got all the caps on the sheet, you got free things. I collected five whole sheets of caps, and I got a free football.

I was working at a BP car wash place, and they just turned to that name. The manager was all right, even taking me a couple times to a NAIA race, the Martinsville, Bristol, and Richmond 500, but I didn't have too much of a fun time because usually Richard Petty won them all. I was an Allison fan. Mom didn't like it too much because they were a little bit older than I was, but I had some great times. I wasn't much into alcohol, but I found marijuana. I chilled real easy.

Mowing the yard one day in a hurry, I had on hard-soled shoes. Walking uphill backward, my foot slipped into the mower. It killed the mower, sliced through the hard sole, and cut up my big toe like a gator mouth. To fix things, I had to go to the hospital and get eight stitches with numbing medicine. Dad said I would raise off the bed with each stitch. Dad said, "I would have slugged him if it were what my dad told me."

Going home to Kentucky at Christmas on I-64, every time I passed it, there was an amusement park in Huntington, West Virginia. And when I saw it, I always reminded me of Marshall, and my heart went out to them and their lost football team and their families.

So Dad got picked up doing eighty-five in a seventy on the freeway in Virginia. I saw the state trooper sitting on the side of the road, and Dad had a 1967 Ford Fairlane. Brother, it had some get up and go to it. I don't know what size engine he had, but it sure could burn some rubber.

I had a pretty good manager and assistant. We got onto the infield once at Richmond 500 when I smelled something I hadn't detected in a while. It brought flashbacks from up in Chi-town. The next-door neighbor was a race car fan. He said he had the first GTO ever made, and its weirdly shaped gas tank was inside the bumper because a square piece of metal was flipped straight to put the gas in. They only made that on just a few cars I know of.

So we, Charles and my neighbor, went to a place called La Crosse, Wisconsin. We could see people warming up their engines, and the neighbor asked Charles and me, "Can you smell the stank of the rubbers off their cars because it has a smell of its own?"

Then there was a shooting in school. Two women got into it. The next day, we had armed cops all down the corridors. When I was going there, they say there were 3,200 to 3,600 students. That's a lot of kids. The absentee list was about three pages long and then five or six pages long in winter. I took care of the cradle robber.

So my big day came finally. Dad wanted to know if I wanted a car.

I said, "Heck, yes! I got cash, so let's go!"

Then I saw my very first car. I bought a black 1941 Oldsmobile with lots of chrome and the very first automatic, he told me Hydra-Matic, I think, with a straight eight cylinders. It wasn't the fastest, but it sure was built, and I do mean solid. I had a truck. I pity someone if he hit on me because I liked my chances better than his. I saw my first live aura on a human face to face, it was like to passing ship, we looked at each other at a glance and went on. I saw this person again with the same aura in 1972, we smiled at each other, ear to ear, at that was it.

When I purchase something, I take really diligent care of it. I compounded it to get the dullness of the color. Then came the wax. Let me tell you. That black stood out. The neighbors on each side watched me clean her up. It was so slick. If you sat on it, you would slide off. Then on the inside, it was so roomy. It was like two king-sized beds, one in front and the other in the back. And there was probably four more in the trunk. Trust me on this because I snuck people inside the drive-in theater, all twelve of us. It was spacey. The seats were cloth material. I think the happiest one of all was Mom because she told me the cradle robber wouldn't be getting me anymore, and she was about correct on that subject. It was real close. I picked up a few students, and then realization set in on me. Three all-women colleges around me, and I saw them everywhere on the plaza and strips roads, that is, thumbing for a ride. The very first two were a blonde and a Indian from out West. We got stoned. And let the good times roll, brother.

I shined my car every two weeks. The only thing I had against the car was that, when it rained and if I were going up a steep hill, the wipers would quit because of something called vacuum wipers. And it was a pain in the ass.

I took a couple people with me, and of course I had the supplies. I ran into one girl and said there was a kid in an old black car. If you wanted to have a fun time, find him because you know how gossip is. It's like a wildfire spreading. I saw the Indian girl again. She said she was graduating this year, and she wanted to go out with a bang. And that was what she got.

Now it was time to take care of the cradle robber, or so Mom called her. I told her I took care of it.

But before I got my driver's license, I taught myself how to drive so I drove in reverse all the time up our street. I got so good that I could back a semi up a gnat's ass with room to spare.

I went to a steak restaurant in town. One of the best manager I ever had was Chuck Hester or Healer. Once he was a trainer for the Lynchburg White Sox, but he was also a black belt in karate. Here I was nailing chicks all over town, but there was a black girl where I worked. She was a really nice women with one child and went to school with me in one class. And she was like ebony, black and shiny.

I didn't think anything about it, but one day, you would see black guys kissing white women, but when a white man kissed a black girl, the picture changed. One day in between class six or seven, guys got me on the stairs and pinned down, telling me not to talk to her again. Message received, loud and clear. I don't understand it, but there a lot of things I don't get.

One day she asked me what was wrong. I told her that some people just couldn't grow up. She quit her job and dropped out of school also.

There was one girl at school. She reeked of odor. I mean, it was like a stench, a smell like you wouldn't believe. It was like a green fog came out of her down there, and I told her I had a connecting I forgot about.

Now the biggest day of my life came. Dad asked if he could adopt me. I said of course. I always thought it was weird our names were different because they ask you for your middle name in school. And of course I didn't have one, so I had to put an "N" in the middle for, I guess, a middle name.

That was when hell came to town, guys. But it was teachers, not the women though. I was called more bad names then. Yes, bastard was the top of the list. Teachers really gave me a tough time.

I fussed to the principal, but that was going in one ear through the other. So I got relocated to another school—rejects, hard knocks, or whatever you wanted to call us—but I didn't have any trouble. It was about 90 percent blacks, but that was great for me because I got more respect from them than anyone was. This is one of the things I have trouble swallowing.

On the weekends, Friday night lights meant football for high schoolers until Sunday morning turf wars, and I don't mean slap on the wrist. It was just plain street fighting. Then on Monday it was high fives and low fives. I just didn't understand it at all.

Before Joel headed off to Iceland, I asked if he knew who my dad was. He said yes. It was a guy named Richard Fields. I found out later that he wasn't my dad, but he gave me his last name because one was considered gutter trash or scum of the earth. That was what people thought back then.

And Joel asked, "What are you going to do?"

I said I would like to meet him, but it never did transpire. It was much later before I found out who my daddy was.

One night getting off work, some couple was getting it on in the parking lot. I mean, he was throwing some good shots on her head, so I thought I could help her out.

I said, "Give the lady a break."

Then I got a smell of alcohol on him, and it was strong. I told him to back off. He threw a punch at me, and he moved like molasses in the wintertime. He tried again, so I gave him a knee lift in his gut, and he dropped to his knees. Then all of a sudden, this woman attacked me. She grabbed me from behind, so I dropped down several to her right. I went to my car, so right then and there, that chivalry didn't exist to me anymore at all. It was dead.

Our cash register lady was really nice. She was about thirty. She had a beautiful car, a 1961 or 1970 Roadrunner, yellow with black stripes and a tail fin. She wanted me, but it never did happen. The last old woman I had was a nightmare from Elm Street. One weekend, we were slow, so she let me drive her Roadrunner around for a time. She picked up a college girl, and we got naked and stoned together. But I had that Roadrunner up to 1,300 miles an hour, and she hung great on the roads.

I always thought I was strong. I found out one night. I just brought me and an eight-track tape, *Paranoid* by Black Sabbath. At the drive-in I went to, the car wouldn't start so here I was, 140 tops, pushing a 1941 Oldsmobile over them little hills at the drive-in, and I thought it was strong for me.

I think the longest number-one rock 'n' roll song was "Joy to the World" by Three Dog Night. They held it for twenty-six weeks, if I am correct.

I think my biggest problems with the male species are that I don't know. I just do transactions with them, like the wind in the willows.

Mom held a lot of Tupperware, Avon, and Home Decorating parties, and I was a natural at it until someone told me it was for gay people. I wasn't going to have this. It was another big mistake in my life, but that was all right, or I wouldn't be alive. Maybe. Who knows?

Dad's Fairlane blew a rod, so he went and bought a 1968 Buick Grand Sport or Skylark California on it. It was red with lots of chrome on the front bumpers. It had a 400 engine in it, and it would squall bad.

Then he bought himself a 1939 Plymouth with four-door suicide doors, so one day I was getting my 1941 worked on. Dad gave me a ride to work, and Greg was in the backseat by himself. He opened the backdoor. It's a good thing we were in town because he fell out. I grasped for him, but it was too late. We were doing about ten to twenty miles an hour when he fell out. His face smacked the pavement, and blood was everywhere. We got to my workplace, and Dad got him all cleaned up. But he caught heck from Mom, no doubt, because there wasn't any seat belts or turn signals in our cars back then.

Then hell came to town. The Minnesota Wrecking Crew came to the Foundry with their cousin Ric Flair the Nature Boy, and I think he stole that "Whew!" sound from me. That was what I always said when they wrestled.

There was a teacher at our school. He was also a cop and a wrestler. Bobby Williams was a pretty decent-sized man. I said I would drop a medicine ball weighing about twenty-five pounds onto his stomach. He was the only cop I ever trusted in my life, so I asked him what the worst accident he ever saw. He told me he was up in Boston, of course the Boston Strangler's home. He went there, and he found a woman killed by him. He broke the broom handle, stuck the woman with the jagged edge of the broom, and shoved it up her vagina. She bled to death, so he asked for a transfer to another city. He was Lynchburg bound.

I was getting close to graduate, but it didn't happen. Dad said I was taking too many study hall classes, and of course he was right. I missed it by two credits, and you could only take one class for summer.

Then realization set in on me. Uncle Sam wanted me. I was screwed dry or wet, any way you cut it. I was drafted. I had to give up all my drugs then. I should have turned into a choirboy and been good. Mom gave me the option of my baseball cards from 1964-1969, I had every baseball card. One Pete Rose rookie card, and two Nolan Ryan baseball cards, and comic books that had every Spider-man book through 1972, and every Hulk book through 1972, and I had the first five, Fantastic 4 comic books. The only reason I bought these books was because of the Thing, and one second edition of the X-men, when professor X battled his brother Jaggernaunt. My option from mom was either to keep all of these mementos from my childhood or get rid of them. She got rid of them.

Dad, a recruiter, got me to enlist in to the navy. One day in the summer, a guy I knew well and I were riding around, and we were burning one joint. I smelled something. Smoke was coming out from under the dash. I told him to put out the joint, but that wasn't it. It was an oil smell. That's right. It was getting ready to throw a rod, and that was what happened.

I was getting ready to go into the service. I didn't need a car, so I borrowed Dad's Buick one night to go to work. But on the way home, there was about a half-mile of pure straightness ahead. I punched it, and when I did, there must have been a lot of carbon built up because I blew the muffler completely off the car. Then I caught hell from Dad, sliding and tearing his car all up. I had to go to a place called Midas Muffler Shop. I blew it up, so I was responsible for the car. It was great to punch that four barrel. I smiled when I blew out of there.

Three other guys joined the service at the same time. One was with me when my car blew up. We joined together on a buddy-buddy plan. I took a class in Operation Specialist, AKA radar man on ship. I never did drugs again.

So here we were off to Great Lakes, Illinois. It was colder than a witch's tit. It was snowing and sleeting, the whole kitchen sink, like when I lost my fingertips and toes.

To me, boot camp wasn't rough. It was boring as hell to me, with paperwork and a lot more paperwork. We couldn't smoke in boot camp unless the petty officer would let us. They were usually chiefs or first classmen. Now my body was like enough electricity to light up Tokyo and New York City all at once.

When I was in boot camp, they make you do a lot of exercises there, especially climbing over this twenty- or thirty-foot wall of straps going up over the top and back down. Some guy got to the top and wouldn't go over on the other side, so I said, "Let's go or get shoved over." I went right around him with no problem because height doesn't bother me at all. I climbed ladders twenty feet high to paint.

Christmas came, so Dad and the family came to pick me up from boot camp for two weeks. We stopped by Dad's sister's house in Chicago, where Betty lived with her husband, a photographer. And all her kids were with them. It was great to see Vicki again. She was more beautiful as ever but six years older. It was probably the last time I would see her. While we were in Chicago it was the last time I would see Vicky Lynn, her brother and sister, because her mother got remarried to a pretty good photographer.

We headed to our hometown for Christmas at Pappy's house, and when we got there, he was watching my boys playing, the silver and black. The Oakland Raiders were on. I saw the part were Stabler rambled in for a touchdown to take the lead, and what happened next was an impossible feat. There is no way he could have caught that ball because I tried it and I have really strong fingers. I couldn't bring it in for a completion. There was no way in hell, but today it is called "the miraculous reception." Like I said, Franco Harris's fingers aren't any stronger than mine are. So he caught it, and they say the rest is history. But on Christmas Day, the undefeated Dolphins played the Chiefs in double overtime before it was decided by a field goal by the Dolphins.

I got back into boot camp again. We only had two more weeks to go. We were going to graduate. First off, my first unit, 513, won the best unit. Then they sent me to 521, and they got the admiral's salute for a weekend pass. I was in 525, a bunch of nobodies, the misfits, renegades, the place I always felt at home.

So I was still in Great Lakes for Operation Specialist School when I was in the two-year program school. Don't count time off. I wasn't going to sixteen weeks of torture. Ain't no way in hell this was going to happen.

When I went off base, I stopped by this jeweler and bought Mom a brooch pin, one whole carat diamond and twenty-four-carat pin for about $300 back then. I say today it's probably worth $2,000, but I love her with all my heart. She was the only one who was always there for me at any time of the day.

I flunked school. So did the other two. We were discharged from school. The fourth one got kicked out because of medical problems. Lucky dog. I went up to Racine, Wisconsin, to get a buzz and watch the Dolphins go undefeated over the Redskins for the Super Bowl.

But the year before that, I was so happy for one guy, Lance Allworth, who was nicknamed Bambi. He would throw a shoulder into you that rocked the safety and linebackers for a loop. He also won with Mike Ditka. There wasn't much on him, but he was a Bear back then.

I was waiting to see where they were going to send me. It was Whitney Island around Seattle, so Dad, a chief now, got me on a father-son program. I got stationed in Norfolk, Virginia, the Little Creek amphibious base for seals. And one of Dad's early years was in Great Lakes. He gave us a tour of the base and told me I'd better be good or they would beat the hell out of me, but in my opinion, that's anywhere you go.

I felt like I was at home stationed at Inshore Undersea Warfare Group (IUWG-2), one badass outfit. I considered them outcasts or rejects. I thought they were a bunch of good fellows. I just wanted my two years up as soon as possible. I was trying to fit in with the crowd, and it didn't take too long. No one really thrilled me. Then a guy from Jeffersonville, Kentucky, around the Louisville area, named John Carey was a seabee. A stalky lad, he was broad and strong.

One day an old drunkard was raising hell in the barracks. He got on my case for being on the phone because he wanted to use it, so he got to me with his mouth. He wanted to hole down with me. That wasn't any problem. I was ready to go a few rounds, but he was drunk. It wouldn't be any problem. This person jumped in.

Carey said, "If you want to fight me …"

He blew in each hand to strike, but he didn't do a thing but go on. But he was the only man I knew who would stand up for me. Then of course, he got shipped to another place for duty. But first we went fishing one day, and another guy he knew in his unit went fishing.

He and I were fishing, catching nothing but bluegills, and he was getting impatient. So I decided to do what Chester told me to do. I cut some bluegills into some strips, and buddy, let me tell you. There wasn't any bite. It was pole heading toward the lake, being pulled in.

I grabbed that rod and landed a fifteen- to twenty-pound blue channel catfish on the line. He was belly button-down length. We ended up catching six of them blue channels, but I had my eyes on something else, a big fish. What it was, I do not know. I hooked him once. Snap went the line. We used some more bluegill snap again. I started having a temper tamper, so I grabbed a twenty-pound test line. I hooked his ass again, and the people I was with, their jaws dropped after they saw the belly on that fish. It looked like one of Ronnie's fish, them buffalo carp he caught in the early sixties. But then he jumped again. Then snap he was gone, and I gave up on it. But we had a good feast on them blue channel catfishes.

Drugs were out of this world all around. If you named it, it was there. After that, I knew my limitations of my temple inside, but thanks for caring. I'm as fine as a person could ever be. I went to town with someone, and what I saw hurt me so bad that I thought I would throw up. On the store window, a sign read "No pets or sailors allowed in here."

I had a lump in my throat that hurt bad because I was so proud of serving my country like Pappy, Dad, Chester, Ronnie, Charles, and Joel. And some municipal places also said to keep pets and sailors off the grass! People I saw decades later said they had seen the same signs I had.

But a few weeks earlier, I watched George Foreman take down Joe Frazier in two rounds of pure hell. It had to be for Smoking Joe. He went down six times. I was like Foreman in the early and mid-1960s. I had the reach on everybody, so I used it to my advantage and get over as quickly as possible because *Sports Illustrated* wrote that a taxi could wait on him and he'd be ready.

I kept to myself because the seabee was gone, so one day I was in the barracks shooting pool in the recreation room when some scruffy-looking guy came in. He looked like he had a hangover. He shot a couple games of pool, and he was good. He had his own cue stick, but Dad bought us a pool table in 1965, and I shot well, especially banking.

So we were chatting, and pot came up. And sure enough, he had some Michael Stone. We called him Stoney from Pittsburgh. We went up to his hometown, and his friends had the best times of their lives with the drugs I had.

One night I had guard duty, and guess who was coming to town? Led Zeppelin was doing their fourth or fifth album. I didn't get to go because, like I said, I had guard duty. I even offered $50 to pull my shift. There were no takers at all, and $50 was a whole lot of money back then. Some didn't even go, but I still stayed behind. Well, maybe next time.

One day some guy hurt himself, and the officers were trying to give it to him good. When you're in the service, they completely own you. If you damage the goods, they will tear you apart. One time, Dad in the late 1950s or early 1960s was getting some sunshine on the ship and fell asleep. He said he was about three to four hours on deck, and he could barely move. So he had to work with severe burns on him in the galley (kitchen) in the service. But when I filled out my benefits, like in case I got killed, everything went to Pappy. Every job I had, Pappy would have got it.

On one weekend right before my birthday, I thought I would drink some before my duty. The next morning, I got myself a half-gallon of Jim Beam. I was winning every game I played. By then, the bottom of the bottle was covered up. I finally lost, so I was going to go to the bathroom. But when I got up, everything went black. They said I landed face-first. I was going to bed after the bathroom. Some guys tried to help me down to my room on the first floor. There were two sections of steps. I told them I was all right. Then I thumped down the stairs, laughing all the time.

Then I said, "I got it this time."

Wrong! Boom I went, again with a thud. At least the steps were over with. Now it was time for my bed. They got me all settled in, and one person asked, "Shouldn't we turn him on his side or belly?" I was glad they did because, before they got out of my room, upchucking was about to begin.

There was like a six-by-six window opening, so I must have thought I could make it do. Wrong! It was all over the screen, windows, and walls. Oh, yeah, it was there for me to clean when I woke up. Some dude took my shift for me, but the worst thing of it all, Mom and the rest came down to visit me on my birthday. I don't remember a darn thing. But I tell you this: no more large quantities like this incident.

I finally liked someone in my life. I would take him home where my parents lived on weekends, and we had a good old time. Some people were getting married a lot around town.

I never did get out of the States, but I did go on a two-week exercise mission. I majored in sensors. We set the bombs on a base called Camp Pickett in Virginia. We blew up one tank. Then tragedy struck on the first weekend. We were having fun until Sunday when everybody was coming back in for the rest of the exercise when a couple people ran off the road, wrecked into a creek, and drowned two soldiers in our outfit.

While I was in there, Stoney asked if we could go in on an apartment. I thought about it and then said sure. I forgot to tell you that Dad bought a station wagon called Kingwood. It was gigantic. It looked like something from outer space. He talked me into purchasing the Grand Sport from him for $1,200. That was a lot of money back then in 1973. We would cruise up and down to Virginia Beach and pick up all kinds of ladies. We met a lots of heads (partiers), that is, and we would race up and down the strip. I dusted them all—Cobra, Vettes, Super Sports, Roadrunners, and the rest of them.

So one day, some old chap pulled up and asked, "Would you like to race?"

I asked, "In that thing?" I thought he hadn't got a prayer.

It happened to turn out that I didn't know when they let cars in America. He dusted me at least one and half. It was called a 1964 Triumph. I mean, that thing couldn't have been no more than three inches off the ground.

We went to Pittsburgh one weekend to party with his friends. I thought I would try to experiment on something, to see how much gas it would take up and back. Gas was starting to be a big hassle to me. If you had an odd number on your license plate, you could get it that day. If not, you had to get it the next day. Gosh!

The speed limit changed from seventy to fifty-five, and to me, that really blew. We went the limit, and it took forty gallons of gas because this car was a beast really. I thought I would try it a little faster, actually a lot quicker. Don't believe everything you hear about saving gas at fifty-five. I didn't get under seventy-five. It was mostly ninety-five. It felt like we were floating, and believe it, I was shocked that it only took twenty-six gallons of gasoline.

One soldier asked if I wanted to go to a concert with him. I said sure. I was sure he was gay, but that never bothered me at all if they kept their hands to themselves. He told me his friend had to pull duty that day. So I went with him, and the band hadn't showed up yet. The crowd was starting to get real moody. Nasty would describe it. They were probably higher than a pine tree. So they sent, I guess, the backup band. And let me tell you. They had the place a rocking and a rolling.

For the second show, the main attraction finally showed up. So they started playing, and it didn't take very long at all. There was hissing, booing, and cursing. Then came the drinks being thrown. He said he would never come back here again. We all didn't care. But I didn't toss anything like that because, to me, that's something to drink.

After we demanded the backup band again, they rocked the arena once more. I never heard of them, but they did, in my opinion, an exceptional performance, the second-best concert that I've ever seen.

I was at home one day. UCLA was playing Notre Dame in basketball. And let me tell you. It was a first fight knockout, Jonnybrook. UCLA was riding an eighty-six game winning streak. I just watched last year's North Carolina State battle of the undefeated. They were on probation the year before and weren't eligible to go, but it was held in St. Louis, a neutral site. But at the very end, UCLA gave all they could. They landed about four shots and three rebounds in about five seconds. Uncle Doug's wife and his wife stopped by. We had no food in the fridge, only booze. It was bachelor life at its best. During this visit Doug told me about this woman from Kentucky and we started writing to each other. She said that her and some people at work witnessed a tornado hit the Ohio river, from the 3rd floor where she was working. It split the Ohio river in half like the Red Sea. Earlier Chester was working in Zenia, Ohio and it was the year of epic tornadoes for that region.

Oh, yeah. One night three other cats were on the prowl, and on a naval base, we had one straightaway. It was about three-fourth of a mile. Higher than all get out, I punched or tromped it. I got up to eighty-five. And the worst thing that could happen did, a MP truck appeared. *Oh, shit*, I thought. *Nope. Here comes the light on top of it.*

I would be busted with weed, pills, coke, and alcohol. It was looking bad. I jumped out of the car real fast, and I mean, real fast. I think I shut the door fast enough to keep the smoke from coming out.

Then he asked, "Going to a fire or something?"

I said, "No, I think there was a missing sound, and I wanted to see if I could find out what it was."

It cost me my base pass for the rest of my stay in the service.

Finally Carla got married to a navy man, so now all my uncles and aunts were all married. And another one was coming into the family, Michele Lynn, our only sister.

My Buick had a problem with it. Something didn't sound good at all, so we all had a great chief. And when they say they are the backbone of the navy, believe it. It's true. They're just like sergeants in the army, the backbones of the service. So go to them, please, for any problems you may have.

He drove it and told me it was the right inner bearing, and he said he would fix it for me. I said great. In sixteen hours, I would be the big twenty and on leave for two weeks. I was getting stoned now with a half-ounce of weed and drinking some beer with it, something with seven ounces in it. We had to go to a car parts place. I went back again, but I guess he must have changed the bearings. They didn't match.

It was about time for my birthday, so I stopped by Carla's crib to see her husband. I didn't know she went back home to Kentucky, so here I was listening to him ramble on. I told him I was on leave and heading home. Some how I got talked into going to Kentucky with him, but first I had to stop by Mom and Dad's first. I think I'm an alien or something, which you will find out later with this book that I have.

I was starting to unwind, thinking the good times were ahead for me. But that wasn't going to happen. I went to sleep at the wheel. I went over the median strip. I crossed both lanes and went into the fields, taking down four pretty small trees, but the last two, it was all over but the shouting. I must have sideswiped the fifth tree because it looked like an accordion. The sixth one stopped me dead cold. I remembered watching lights coming to me. Then I passed out again.

Meanwhile here was my uncle in the backseat, passed out, but he was on the floorboard of the car because he couldn't party that good. After two joints and six beers, he was out for the night. When I woke up this time, I saw a big, bright light shining in my big blue eyes. I saw the doctor doing something to me. Then I passed out again. What a hell of a birthday party. The Lord was with me. A stranger took my weed, beer, and eight-track. Thank you, stranger, because it saved me. I slept in the car that night with my uncle, so when I woke up, he was gone. He was AWOL. You couldn't be sure.

The sheriff greeted me with a big smile, but that was a disguise. He wanted to bust me bad, but some nice person saw me run off the road and checked if I were all right. I was out, so being my uncle, he took all my case and a half of beer, a half-ounce of weed, and my eight-track stereo. He said I must have an angel over my shoulder. I think he might be right.

Here I was, bloody as all get out, thumbing for a ride. I cleared my head, called the base, and told them where I was. They came and got me, and I canceled my leave.

One day out of the blue, Charles was telling me about a girl from Kentucky, that he knew where she lived. He asked if it were all right for her to write, so I agreed that she could. She wrote for about a month, and I couldn't handle this crap. It was over really fast. I drove a one-and-a-half-ton truck out of the gate by a little creek straight out on that road, and on the way back, I saw how fast I could go. Like I said, I scanned everything, and I reached eighty once. And if someone pulled out into my lane, I would drop it into second gear and hope it didn't flip over.

The first time the Lord told me not to smoke that joint, the one Pat gave me to light, I said, "No."

He asked, "Why?"

I told him, "We are going to get pulled over."

The next town, we got pulled over. Now you know the rest is history. I was back on the base again, watching the Buffalo Bills beat the Oakland Raiders. My team got there first to Monday Night Football. The receiver who really killed them, he changed his name to Rashad, and later he was a good receiver. I was extremely passionate for sports, but I was on the team's backs. Take my dad, for instance. I think he got his rocks off when someone got hurt. It's barbaric, I think.

I was chilling, thinking of what to do when I got out of this two years of madness I was in. What about being a gun for his? Narcotics? I still didn't know. I decided I would start working out again at the naval gym. It was gigantic and everything. It was too huge for me because, like I told you earlier, I am a rogue.

My expectation was like no other. It was grueling. I established fighting in the suburbs of LA, San Diego, and Chicago. I told you I was hungry for survival and knowledge, and what I finally figured out what I was missing in life was being a kid. I had no childhood. I also found out that I was the best observer in the world. I scanned the entire environment, just like the Terminator, and I always expected the unexpected because you never know what's over the horizon.

Then I tell you. Talk serious to him because that student is going through hell. I moved around a lot, and it's the same all over. Talk to him or her. Talk to him or her about it. Bullying has been around since the beginning, and it will always be there.

So I had a duty job one day. I was loading railroad rocks onto a truck. We had three people but two shovels. So I said, "Let's go," but we backed up the truck against the mounds of rock. I started using my hands. It wasn't too hot today at least.

Running my hands and fingers in there gave me a great idea. I almost shoved out two people with one, and I nearly had the same load as them with my hands. I started digging into them rocks, so I started doing this regularly. I had busted skin and split nails that were more purple than any.

Some guy wanted to know if I wanted to play a game call racquetball.

I asked, "What's that?"

But I found out. But the game reeks. Of course that's my opinion.

Yeah, what a great facility they had on the base. It was wonderful. But this gym was great.

When I was going out the door, I thought I would try leg press. Mom called them "sexy legs," and that would embarrass me. I didn't do much weights, so I gave it a try. I put it at five hundred pounds. No problem. And at 145, I was impressed with it. So with 750 pounds,

I barely got it there. It was good enough for me. I was thinking about the days of pushing around my 1941.

I was persuaded to move in with him and two others. I mean, we partied hard. By the time I woke up, I had let my head down. They sent me to a psychologist to be checked out. I told them I just wanted to drink. He stamped it, and I was gone like the wind in the willow.

There was two and a half months to go. I kept myself in tip-top shape, so one day, chief told us to move some curbstones, the thing that kept your car from moving. They weighed about three hundred to four hundred pounds, so I and another guy were moving them.

Captain stopped by and hollered, "You want to toss some horseshoes at lunch."

Both of us are Kentuckians, so we said sure. Let me tell you. He was damn good. We were still moving curbs when his slipped out of his hands and left me to hold my end.

He told me, "Sorry."

I said, "Just pick it up, and let's go."

He looked like he had hell the last night. So lunch came, and we started tossing. Like I said, he was good. He won the base's tournament a few times. We were chatting, but when I went down to pick up my horseshoe, I didn't get back up. It was like I was in a fetal position. They called medic (doctors) and took me to Portsmouth, the huge hospital. I was laid up for about two weeks with narcotics in my system and chilling out, wondering if everything were going to be all right now.

I got back onto my feet. I had a month and a half to go. Some head stopped by, asking if anybody wanted to buy a car. I asked how much. It was $75 for a 1964 Corvair Spider. It was a four-speed, almost the ugliest car I had ever seen. It looked like they took a paint roller to it. I was getting tired of walking all of us, so I said sure and put the title in my hand.

Remember, I talked about the doctor visiting earlier in my childhood. I threw my sandwich into the air, and it stuck to the ceiling, but under the stain on the ceiling where Margaret and Chester got married. Then my mom and dad got married in the same spot, along with Iantha and Ronnie and Pat and Carla. This was the spot I also married Janet, the mother of my only daughter, Wendy Sue.

Then about that time, the chick my uncle told me about wrote again. I was thinking about being here over two years with everybody back at home married, so we kept on writing until I got out. I got out and had to go to court on my last day for speeding in my Corvair, forty-seven in a thirty-five. I was getting stoned to the bone. I was out of the service. I was a civilian again. I got home. The girl in Kentucky said she would like to meet me, so I went to a town called Olive Hill by a bus depot.

I ended up marrying her, the girl from Kentucky, that my uncle Doug had told me about, and then the nightmares started to begin. We lived with Mom, and Dad. I got me a job at Overhead Doors. The owner was a navy man who liked to serve his country. Dad had recruited him. Like Mom said, he was charming, using his hands to talk, so maybe it's a gift.

Dad talked me into bowling on a team with him for the rest of the season. Pappy and Doug took me to an erotic movie, and I came home and impregnated my wife. And Wendy Sue was born. Well, let me tell you. Remember when I said they would all be married. Wrong! The horns came out. Jealous with envy, she took it out on me. There were fingernail marks on my arms, and Mom saw it. The levee broke. I must say I never had another scratch on my body.

So I knew what I had to do, to get out of Virginia or die. You got it. I went to my hometown again. The reason was that Pappy and Mamaw lived there, but before we moved, John Wooten of UCLA was retiring from coaching. And who did they play? Of course, Kentucky in the finals of the NCAA tournament.

Mom made my favorite dish for supper. Then something hit me like a two-by-four up against my head. I came home from work. I was starting to eat when Mom said Alvin had to be put under. He had a tumor on his right rear leg. She said he howled awful this morning. She called Dad and had to take him to the vet's.

That was the first death that rocked my world. It was a burning sensation in my inners. I felt like crying, but I did not. But I couldn't eat anything until the next day. Dad got a two-year deal at the vocational school with pay.

I took auto mechanics, which I was pretty good at, especially tune-ups. To me, it was all in the cars. The teacher's name was Thomas Jefferson, and he was a good teacher. My instructor always called me "Swifty" because I did my job so quickly, but I always got the job done right. Larry and I in vocational school heard a man talking about an Asian, who had a heart punch that could kill you after five steps. He asked me, "what do you think about that myth? I replied, "I don't know Larry, the Lord can part the Red sea so anything is possible". So in a movie I watched in 2003, that I watched called Kill Bill 2, then I really wondered.

So now my wife was pregnant with soon-to-be Wendy Sue. I'm getting ahead of myself again. Chester ran a restaurant during this time in Ripley, Ohio. He had a brother named Morris, the best carburetor man I've ever known. He ran the garage next door, so Chester and Morris wanted out of the business. Chester wanted to go drive semis, and Morris went to Miami, Florida. I remember Morris when I was knee high, and he had two great cars, just like Marvin would do on his 304 Ford Fairlane 55 model.

When I was eight or nine, Morris was working on a car and asked me which one I liked the best. I said that one. He also had a grin on him, like Paul Newman with curly hair too.

Dad ran the restaurant at the garage for two years. I was doing great at mechanical jobs. I was troubleshooting and buying all kind of tools for jobs. I bought a timing light. I didn't really use it much. I always went by sound. I was figuring things out though, like why I was paying a man $75 a month to do my paperwork. He didn't take to it very kindly, but like Pappy would say, he'd be all right when the swelling went down.

So here it was Thanksgiving Day, on November 27, 1975. The day before, the wife had a fake delivery, so I said, if it were a boy, I was going to name him Turkey, like the old gent that hung around here in the morning. So I had her pumping gasoline on Thanksgiving, but that night, twenty minutes past midnight, on November 28th, 1975, my one and only daughter, Wendy Sue, was born. I hired in-laws and uncles to work for me, along with the local guy who had been there since the 1950s.

She had blonde hair like corn. Let me tell you. People, you don't make much money at all in gasoline because there's so much taxes on it. You might make four cents on a gallon. The worst job I ever had to do was put one nut on a 1974 Porsche clutch. I couldn't see it, but I had to feel for it.

One day I was moving this engine block out of my way when reality hit me really hard again. My back went out again, and I still get it today. Now her dad was a good soul. Lots of people didn't care for him, but I did, and so did Wendy Sue, my sidekick, you might say. I was doing a tune-up on a car one day when some pain started to get bad. I had to give up school and the garage too. Her dad John was a car collector and a heavy equipment operator, just like I did in the service. He had a 1976 Plymouth Fury I wanted to get my claws into, but there was a knocking in it. He thought it was maybe a loose piston pin.

John got me to start watching *The Gong Show*. Something he liked to do was sell junk so he got me to watch *Sanford and Son* as well. Sad to say, I still watch these old shows today and think about him fondly.

Then he told about this white convertible 1964 Pontiac Catalina. He said it really gripped the pavement. So the narcotics were helping a lot of the pain go away for a while, but during this time my wife was emotionally and verbally killing me and trying to drive me insane all because I was down sick and she had to work.

So just about Memorial Day, I couldn't stand it anymore. I spent the night away with a student at school to go and see *King Kong* with Jessica Lange in it. I'd been getting high for almost a year again. My wife from Kentucky and her brother went looking for me and found me in Manchester, Ohio, with her. On the way home, I told her it was over between us. She said things like sleeping with my friends younger brother, thinking bad thoughts and things, that weren't true at all. I got onto the corner of the street. Her mom, brother, and sister were loading up the truck. She wouldn't get out, so I helped by kicking her out the passenger door in a 1974 Vega station wagon.

Then she finally got out, and I told her to take it easy on Wendy Sue, but she said she was going to make it a living hell. And that she did, my people. That she did. At first, to me, it was like an adult chicken hawk swooped down and snatched her up, and it was over. The feeling was like Alvin's death, a burning feeling. I cried many of nights in my house in the Vega for four months, yes I was homeless I had to live in my car for four months. I was chauffeur for people trafficking just about anything you can name in Cleveland, Columbus, Cincinnati, and little towns you wouldn't even think about. I couldn't get any other jobs at this time because of my disability, believe you and me I tried and tried, but this was it. I know it was the people I drove around were doing bad things, but I was desperate for money and some pain relief.

I caught word in the air that Pappy saw the light. He was at the kitchen table at lunch. Normally he always sat straight across from where he also sat. The thunderstorm blew in a good one. A bolt of lightning struck and hit, but if he were sitting normally, he would have been toasted.

So I would live off the land. I had an Ambassador fishing reel. Let me tell you what a badass reel it was. It was an open-face reel.

I stayed at a person's crib. Someone had passed out on me, so I went to go and get my car. Someone broke into it, and he took my rod and reel. Now what? So Pappy's dunking (baptism) was coming up, so I made it in plenty of time. I talked a long time with the preacher, talking how come I didn't come to church anymore, the reason I hadn't been to church was because of hypocrites, dress codes, drama, and gossipers, and when I come back I will be wearing t-shirts and blue jeans, and I still were them today to church, and will to my dying days.

So I told him, and you should have seen his face. It was totally baffled. Blank, you name it. That would have been right. Then I started coming back to church again. He died about eight years after that. When I came back, the sheriff was waiting for me with the papers for divorce.

The year before was the very first time I didn't have Wendy Sue with me, but a hell of a lot more was probably coming. I was doing tobacco cutting and hanging it in the barn. I liked the bottom rail because I wanted the man or woman to sweat like the rest of us. Right on the top rail was right next to the heat of tin. I made a pretty good name for myself.

Right now I am feeling good because I'm really the nicest person that anyone could meet. I just wish I had time to just talk to someone. It's first priceless to me. I was a security cop in Lexington, Kentucky. I came home one day and Dugan's Valley, right outside of Kentucky, there were five funnel clouds going across the hillside. I was in a 1974 Pinto, the car that if it was rear ended it would explode on you. So, after seeing the funnel clouds I floored it coming down the hill. I was doing 80 to 90 mpg thinking I could punch through the funnel cloud, like an arrow shooting through it. By the time I got through the funnel cloud I was doing 25 mph and I was starting to sweat! Praise the Lord I say! And a few weeks later I was drinking and had a flat tire, and continued to drive around on the rim over eight miles into the countryside with sparks just a flying, from the rim meeting the concrete, sparks flying everywhere. Praise the Lord I made it home Alive!!

Meanwhile I got a call from unemployment office. They told me to go to a furniture store in the downtown section. I got in there, and I tell you what. I thought I was homely, but this cat looked like hell warmed over. I will never forget his name, John Harvey. I mean, I felt like Prince Charming. He told me later that there was no way in hell he was going to make it. I moved so much in my time that I could do it in my sleep with a little U-Haul on the back trailer hook. I thought the same thing about him.

We started hanging out at bars. They were calling us Salt and Pepper at work. Now downtown folks, we met all kinds of ladies. It was like picking grapes sometimes. There were three just in a house or some four-apartment sections. We kept three of them busy, so I needed a car, and that was what the doctor ordered. I bought me a 1971 New Yorker, and it was beautiful with no dents or rust at all. It had deep green seats. It was in beautiful shape. John bought a new 1978 Cordova or something like that, white and pretty. It had a 440 engine in it. It was $700, and to me, that was a lot with child support too. I was smoking the highways, baby. I waxed that baby four times a year. It was my car.

Marvin, Junior, Carla, and Pat were drinking one day while Junior went to the bathroom. Carla had a crying fit. During this time, Junior came out and saw his wife crying, and he thought that Marvin had caused the upset. Marvin told Junior he would cut out his gizzard, and they were about to clash when Carla stepped in. She said she was sorry. She wasn't sad about that. Because of almost killing Junior, Marvin never touched another drop after that day.

Then I met a real beautiful woman named Sandra, and that was what she was. It could have worked, but she didn't want me to work.

John asked one day, "Are you crazy?"

So times got hard for money again. I was laid off from work. The girls I knew introduced me to her. It's always friends and more friends when it comes to matchmaking. I met a kid named Timmy in 1974. He was slender and didn't have a big head like mine. I went to his house where he usually smoked with me. He had been in a car wreck that left him paralyzed from the neck down, but he was still a good guy. My cousin Jeff, stopped by to ask me to follow him home in his Camaro. It had been raining a lot, and in route to his house there was a car going really slow, and Jeff and I started to go around him. During this time Jeff spun side ways in his Camaro and I spun to miss him but with a heavy car like this on icy roads, it's a nightmare. Straight ahead lied a 20 foot or more creek drop off into a creek with highwater. But the Lord was with me because I seen three 3 feet high concrete pillars, I thought I would hit them and I tried to stop my momentum to keep from going over the drop off. I shattered the concrete, did a 180 degree turn, the car was steaming, and I didn't see Jeff anywhere. I figured Jeff must have went on home, so I went on home and pulled into the back of my driveway where the auto body shop was. My landlord at the time just happened to be an auto body man. The next day, Jeff came back and wondered what happened and I told him. So he helped me pull my lower grill out of my engine. After doing the grill out of my engine we decided to drive back to where I had wrecked at and I was amazed at what I saw. The concrete pillar I had hit had an I beam in it, covered with concrete, which explained the way I had stopped having done a 180 degree turn. The I beam I hit so hard, had knocked it at a 45 degree angle. After this incident I took the radiator to the shop for repair, the guy said he could fix it and he did. Then my landlord said, Alvin you're A-frame is cracked in half.. he said I Can fix that for you, since hes a body man. I asked how much? He replied $100. I said fix it. It looked brand new afterwards. Jeff and I followed his new stepdad to Fort Thomas Kentucky in his new El Camino. He was following a car that was driving like a snail, so he decided to pass as did I then I thought I'd kick my 318 engine in, and that front end reared up like a Cobra, I said Shit that's a 360 under the hood, not a 318! After passing that El Camino I got to Fort Thomas and I decided to look under the hood, and I smiled from ear to ear and I believe it would have taken a jack hammer to get that smile off my face. Under the hood was a 440 engine.

In 1983, it was the last time I took or used any acid, LSD because it ain't worth a crap today. I buy weed now just for pain and ONLY for ME!! I'm not a big alcohol dude, it just takes to much for me.

Now Mamaw was trying to be matchmaker or something, but I did meet one girl. She and I just got tested from a scare. Something called AIDS hit the scene. I was clean as a new whistle. I got a job as a cashier at a gas station. I ran into a woman who hooked me up. The next thing you know, I got another one cooking in the oven. Ellery Wyatt was about to be born.

I got married. I got a job. I had to leave so I took this abuse for about a year and a half, and I couldn't stand it anymore. Right, I was divorced again. I had fines and child support to pay. I had no car or license either. I had DUIs, three of them. I had a little money for me from the VA pension check. So sometimes I'd get toasted, wake up, and find out I had wet the bed. Oh, man, this was embarrassing. This happened for about three years. I decided maybe I should quit drinking if I were going to do this.

I went fishing with a guy who was a preacher, and he told me a remedy for being horned by a catfish. And trust me. It hurts like hell. He told me that you take the catfish that horned you and rub it on its belly, and the pain will go away. Believe me when I say it works. Gary asked if I wanted to go to Queen City, or Cincinnati as we know it. I said sure, but I had to bring Ellery back by nine o'clock.

So westbound on 52, the Lord hollered at me again about an eastbound car passing vehicles about a half-mile ahead or more, driving crazily ahead of me. We were doing fifty-five miles per hour in his Cordova. Traffic was stopping in the other guy's lane for yard sales. I knew the other man would not stop in time. The only person who could see it was me in the passenger seat. Ellery was between my legs. Then I snatched the steering wheel from Gary's hands. Then in thousandths of a second, you'd be surprised you can see. He slid into our lane. It was just a hatchback. It split our car in half, and it landed about thirty feet from the road. I saw this guy pressed up against his rear window as he passed us. He pressed it so hard that the windshield came to me, shattering everywhere. Gary ended up getting a few stitches in his left brow. We had completely done a 180-degree turn twenty feet off the shoulder. Ellery got a sliver of glass in his pinky. I had a head full of glass. I had to end up shaving off all my hair to get rid of all the glass in my hair. The local tower said he had never seen anything like that, a car being completely cut in half.

The guy's engine was heading eastbound, but the body part of the car was way off the shoulder. The tower said the car still started, which was weird. But my main concern came when the insurance agent came. I asked about the man from the other car. I inquired as to whether he had lived or died.

He said yes. He had lived, but it took over 140 stitches to close up the guy from the accident. It was a relief off my mind that he lived, but if it were me, I knew I would still be having nightmares to this day from this wreck. Gary's side of the car was up against the firewall.

When the Raiders played the Redskins, I told my cousin I would give him twenty-eight points. He said fourteen would do. They won by twenty-nine points, and he still talks about it today.

It was now October 20, 1986. Let's get down to brass tacks, like they say in the service. Like I said, I got religion real young at seven years old. I didn't understand too much until I was thirty-two years old, when I really opened my eyes forever. I know that God answered my call in 1964 when I prayed for defending myself out in California, when he guided my punches in all my brawls out West.

One thing I do know. I was born with an acne problem. Still today it's bad. I have to take infection pills to battle my oily body for the last two years. If not, my whole body would be nothing but boils and pimples, but before I got the medicine in me, sometimes I get like seven to ten boils on just my head. When I read about poor old Job in the Bible, I really feel lucky that it wasn't as bad as his.

I'm an extremely religious freak, so when Greg had his seventh birthday, I asked what he was reading, and he told me. It was called "the Book." It was translated from the Bible so a moron like me could understand it. I sure did get it in my blood. Greg told me about three years earlier that he couldn't touch the bottom of my shoes in religion, but now I make preachers walk away with their tails between their legs.

I learned something from my Sunday school teacher, Kenny Foreman, one day. He was a preacher at our church. He said he prayed every morning before his feet hit the ground. Well, so did I from that day on. He would ask me how did it read in the Book. Bam! Everybody understood the verse that was printed in the Sunday school book.

One day Greg was going around with members of the church, trying to get people to go, so he stopped by my only friend on earth I ever had, John Harvey Gibbs. Greg asked him about Jesus. He replied he'd never heard of him, and he was almost sixty years old. He heard of God but not Jesus. One of the main reasons I am writing this is because, if I can save one more life in religion, I will do it.

One thing I learned was never to brag. I don't believe in it because I think God would strike me down dead. So every night I have gone to bed for the last twenty-eight years, I say three prayers. First, I say the Lord's Prayer.

I next say, "Bless you for a wonderful and glorious day. May the next day and the day after be just as glorious and wonderful. Bless you for the food we nourished today. Bless our folks, families, and everyone else. I ask for these things in the name of our Father, the Son, and the Holy Ghost. Amen!"

Finally I say, "Bless you for your precious blood, for dying for all us sinners. Forgive those who sinned today, and forgive me for my thoughts. Bless all the nations throughout the land. May there be peace throughout the land. Bless all the churches throughout the land. May the congregation believe in you as I do. Bless you for guiding us to and from today. Bless the sick, the elderly, and the disabled. Bless those who lost loved ones today. Rejoice for all the newborns. I ask for these things in the name of our Father, the Son, and the Holy Ghost. Amen!"

I helped save a few people in my time, but if I can save one more, Amen!

If the Book contradicts just one time, I throw it in the garbage can. But sometimes I fall asleep before I finish my prayers, but at least I was thinking of Jesus, my Savior. It is relentless for me to say, "Thank you, J.C., for everything." If I cook, shave, go, and do anything, thank you, J.C.

When I was a teenager, about 22 to 30 percent believed in the spirit, but my opinion is about 50 to 60 percent believe today. Yes, I started on the Book on October 20. There are a few more October 20 coming up. Weird, isn't it? I recommend to everybody I know, "Just read the first five books of the New Testament: Matthew, Mark, Luke, John, and Acts. And trust me. You will understand it."

The Old Testament is great to read about history. The only story that made me bawl like a baby was Abraham having to sacrifice his son Isaac because I had a son and that would be hard to swallow for me.

In 1987, a Sunday school teacher asked me how it was read in the Book. And everyone in the classroom really understood it.

In 1988, my grandma from Kansas City died. I was in jail and couldn't get out to go to the funeral. I owed $1,800 in DUIs. Frankly for the first and last time, I was drunk. And in between, the law always has your number and will always pull you over to check you, but I didn't have anything to worry about because I never drank again.

So I was at the bottom of the barrel and went to some vineyard restaurant, where they made grape wine there. I went in there with a tank top; shorts showing my sexy legs, as Mom called them; and a pair of scandals on.

Mary Moyer was the owner of the place. They came from the western part of Texas, and she was proud of it. She was a spunky little character. It was a scorcher this year, though he said it was about like this in his homeland. It was dry and great for grapes. He was talking about West Texas State beating Kentucky in 1966. I heard he had his picture taken with old blood and guts, George Patton himself.

So like I said, it was a scorcher, and the chef was a really nice man from Tampa, Florida. I'm sure he was gay. He learned how to do things really fast for gourmet cooking. We were two knockouts.

I almost forgot a really important part in 1981. John and I went out with some ladies and went to the local bar, having a great ol' time. I was kissing this lady passionately. I went to the bathroom and came back. She was all over him. Like I said, I wasn't feeling any pain.

I cursed him out bad, and then I stormed out of there with my New Yorker. I went in next day, and I have a gift of reading people's feelings. I don't like it, but what can I say? He laid into me verbally, which I deserved, but just at that instant, something floored me. I got myself a really loyal friend. Stoney was a great guy, but John, I was proud to call him friend. So Dad, that's one. If I needed him, he would be there. Just like me, he was trustworthy, and he would come and get me on work release.

I knew the jailer, Lloyd Berry, for many years. I make things like Dutch apple pie like Mamaw made it. So here we are getting hammered down with business. One night I prayed a woman would come back into my life. In early June, I asked if he would send me a redhead. I never had one, so I was willing to give it a try.

It was another 100-degree day in June. My first cousin was getting married. She was the one I made her navel bleed. It was about 112 degrees, so I just started working. I couldn't take off for a wedding. But in around the boiler area, it was a nightmare at 150 degrees. Sweat was just dripping everywhere. If you looked down, your glasses would slide off your face. It was just awful in there that night.

Someone quit. It was too hot for him, so Dino the manager asked me, "Who do you want to hire for as a cook? Some man or this woman who has been in the navy?"

Since I was a navy man myself, I said to hire her.

Then he replied, "I figured you would choose her."

So that was the first time I hired someone before. Hell, I think it had been over forty days since it rained, and she was the last one I ever hired.

So just all a sudden, the new cook brought rain with her because I tell you that it poured like the old saying, "cats and dogs," out there. And the old folklore says, like Sandra, Judy told me that, the first time she ever saw me, I was wearing a bandana on my head to keep hair off the food. And when she saw me, she thought I had a steel plate in my head. Judy went back toward the dishwasher, and I told her to get over here before I put this size 10 EEE boot up her crack. After that, she was the greatest worker I ever hired.

Another thing I learned from Sandra was that, if it rains on a Monday, it will rain three more times that week. And 90 percent of the time since 1980, I've been keeping with it. Maybe seven times it didn't do it.

I started getting to know people. Several people I knew were still around from 1976 to now in 1989. The new cook told me she was stationed over in Scotland with her husband. He was also in the service. He was a lifer for twenty years and had five more to go in Maryland. I think that was where he was.

It was Ohio State Fair time in Columbus, but the employees were having a big party for the weekend, and that was what we did. We were riding go-carts, playing horseshoes and volleyball, and doing all the works, especially, you got it, getting stoned. We gave $10 to a vagabond so he could get himself something to eat at the backdoor.

Judy said, "You know he's going to drink that up."

I told her that wasn't for me to decide. I did my job by giving him some money. In other words, my heart and conscience were clear.

They were going to throw a Back to College Days party. It was about to begin. The dessert woman said something to me like, "I think she likes you a lot."

I thought, *Who in the hell is she talking about, woman?*

I thought it must have been a waitress, cashier, or busgirl.

"No," she said. "Judy does."

Well, my jaw dropped to the floor when she told me that. I said, "There's no way in hell."

Like I said, I'm naïve, buddy. I wouldn't know a come-on line if it bit me on my ass.

I didn't have any way to get there, so I said, "I don't have a way there.:

Peggy, the dessert lady, said, "Judy would probably pick you up and take you."

But I thought, *Well, if she wants to, sure.*

The next day she was there, and she picked up two more females. She didn't get high, so I respect that out of people who don't. I walked to the back of the house and got toasted. It was on to the party stop to get me a case of beer, Michelob, I think. Then Judy told the women how sexy my legs were. Well, I blushed a little. Actually a lot. We left to go home, but she wanted to stop by and see Peggy for a couple cups of good coffee.

So all I did was drink and party all I can and learned that my boys had a curse on them that I never knew. Talk about a mind blower. Guess what? That's right. I urinated in the bed again. This was crazy. I passed out drunk so I decided I'd just stay in and drink. WI was doing good until I started drinking a pint of vodka, a 100-proof drink. I drank it all in forty minutes. I passed out, but I didn't piss the bed now.

Judy talked me into going to college for cooking, so I said sure. There was all this delicious food here. I mean, there were some fancy dishes. We went to a bar one night again to call it a weekend, and she had swept me off my feet. Oh, yeah, I forgot to tell y'all. She was a redhead. So now as we know, the Lord does listen to me. Trust me.

She said her husband had been cheating on her for a while. She had two girls, Lena and Gwendolyn, and lost two at childbirth inside the womb.

One day Ellery asked me a question, wondering who Wendy on my Zippo cigarette lighter I bought in 1978 was.

I said, "Maybe someday you might meet her." I was serious. He might.

You know, it's funny what you ask for. Sometimes it could get scary what you ask for. So we started seeing each other, and we finally graduated in 1989 from Hershey, Pennsylvania. Her parents were from Amish country up around Smithville, Ohio. We cooked for all the Clooneys, Heather Renee French, and a few other celebrities who came through and lived in our town. Like I said, we had some great food to cook with. You want it; they have it for you.

Peggy and I were making some dynamite desserts, and the manager said something I didn't like because he was jealous. And because of his remark, I never made another dessert again in a restaurant, only at home.

Her brother and youngest sister moved down with her parents. He was raised in the Amish ways, so he decided it was time to go against their ways and move onward.

She got divorced in December 1989, and I quit drinking on January 1, 1990. I was hungover, but I quit. I didn't take another drink until twenty-two years later. We were watching the Oilers and the Bills play in Buffalo. They were trailing by thirty points, I think, at halftime, and I thought, *If they were going to make their move, it would have to be fast.*

Warren Moon was just lighting it up in Buffalo, but before you knew it, it was a tie game. Buffalo finally won it and went to the Super Bowl. And that was when it happened again, a loss in the Super Bowl, like the last time when the Jets ousted the Colts by nine, which writers said that shocked football. Norwood missed it by quite a bit to me.

So here we were, kicking some tail at Moyer's Vineyard in Manchester, Ohio. I think they liked me up there on their land here in Ohio. I thought I'd grow some vegetables this year, some corn on the cob on about a quarter of an acre, but the hens across the lane ate every silver queen corn seed.

But two weeks before I straightened out my life from drinking, I thought I would sneak out and get drunk. But it was a slow night, so I decided I'd go home early. When I went to bed, I discovered something. I was toasted, but then it hit me. All the time I thought I was peeing the bed, it was Joshua wetting it for me, right in the center of the bed. When I lay down, my pillow was soaked in piss. Man, I was so irate, I couldn't see straight. I nailed him right in the ribs, and I knew it had to hurt.

Mom was screaming, "What's going on in there?"

They thought it was a great joke that he was doing to me, but it was really a great relief that I wasn't.

I purchased a snowball white 1978 Firebird from her brother Wayne. It was mine now with a big firebird on the hood. It had a rubber T-top. It was in excellent shape and had headers on it where someone hand-painted the firebird. It was blue with nice mag wheels. It was a head turner. You know what I mean.

Then one day Judy got out her measuring ruler from her sewing kit, and I tell you what. I was awed. I was stunned about what she told me. I said there was no way. Then she said some Holmes guy got nothing on your big boy. Not at all.

Well, I felt like cheap dirt all the time. I thought it was drugs, cars, and money. I was just simply, in my opinion, abused. All the women I had told me that, but I thought, *Yeah, yeah, yeah, if you say so.* I always told you I wouldn't know a compliment if it slapped me upside my head. And yes, I was naïve.

But that's enough about that. We were going to take Ellery back to his mom one night, and Wayne said he would like to go and get out for a while. I said sure. We went to Pappy's house, where Ellery only lived four houses down. Marvin and Teresa were staying with them after his wife took her own life. So Wayne saw her as well.

That was all it took. When we got home, Wayne came over and talked about Teresa's life, if she ever did any drugs or drink. No, not Teresa. He asked if he could get her phone number from me.

I thought about it and said yes. Judy was sitting beside me on the walkaround pool we had, and Wayne took off to call her. Then I laid down the facts to Judy that we would probably be moving soon. She asked why. His dad and Judy had, like I said before, Amish in their blood. The Lord told me that, when I gave him this phone number, things were going to change. I told Judy what I heard, and she said there was no way! I said okay, but she was wrong. And I was right.

She said, "Explain yourself."

Then I told her about all my past, which she knew already, but with him being Amish, there was no way in hell. Well, you might be wrong because she knew I had good senses about things like that. From the richest to the poorest people, it's still all the same, but just the time, just like it always has been through life. Well, guess what? I was the best man. But Judy's sister said Tim Daulton was about one of the greatest man I have ever met. He's as funny as you can get and like me. He always respects people.

The big day was here. I was best man, and Judy was best women. I guess that's what it's called. Like I said, I'm the butcher of the English language. Judy was working really hard so everything would go great for the reception.

Well, guess again, people. It was a really sweltering day. Judy was feeling faint. As the preacher was talking, she was getting paler and paler. I rushed over there to grab her. I clinched her by my side, holding on to her. We were going outside the doors with cameras rolling. Wayne was wondering what was going on. So it was all over now. They were heading for Niagara Falls for their honeymoon. Amen.

But right before I moved up to God's country, some teenage thugs were going around, raising heck around the trailer court. I was drinking some and just chilling. They came my way, sitting on the trunk of my dad's car. You know what I mean. I was having an unmanageably bad hair day. It was getting ready to explode right here. They smarted off. Bam! After three licks, three went down. The fourth one ran like the speed of light.

Mom came running out. "What's going on out there?"

"Taking the trash out, Mom."

"Well, be a little quieter, please."

Judy and I had a great relationship, so if I said I were going to my throne, that was what I was using it for, but if I said I were going to my office, I was getting stoned.

I was smoking rubber left to right. The owner didn't like it very well, but the staff loved it, especially the fakeness.

So like I said, they got back from their honeymoon right away. The Lord's senses took over with a big jump. Keep a close eye on this. About a month later, the girls, Lena and Gwendolyn, were at their grandparents' house. No one answered the door, so I stuck my head in and heard no answer. I told them they weren't far away. Later I found out I was breaking into the house.

So the next day, I picked up the girls.

Their dad said, "This is God's country, and I'm God. So you call next time before you come."

Well, my jaw dropped to the floorboard.

Then when we were pulling away, Lena, a brilliant girl, asked, "Did I hear what I just heard?"

But Gwen was a little slow. Probably a playground was in her mind.

We said, "I can't believe that comment he made."

Judy, losing her insanity, was being held up at their farmhouse. Like I said, you could come up if you called, but Judy called me. She told me to come and visit. I mean, you could cut the air with a knife right now. I told her I had to get ready for work, like they had it planned that way.

On a Saturday, Wayne came down with a piece of paper, written by their dad, telling me they wanted me off the land. You should know I wasn't going to leave Judy up there. I was burning up with rage.

I called Dad and said, "Don't get stupid and go and hurt someone."

He told me to calm down and call the sheriff's office. I did. They replied and said they had one on the way there now.

Judy made one phone call, and that was shocking news. But she called the sheriff's office. They were going up the driveway with dust flying. I saw Judy walking down the driveway and heard complete shock in her voice. We grabbed everything we could. We had to let the pets stay. It was only Shadow we had, and he was a damn smart dog, a black Lab. Dad let us stay for however long we wanted. Thank goodness for parents sometimes.

She was telling us everything, but I think she was holding back on some of them. They tried holding her down on the bed, saying, "Everything will be all right, honey."

So here I was left to do everything. Judy was flipping out because she didn't have a job.

I said I'd take care of everything, so to move our trailer, I stopped by a place in Manchester. He moved it for the swimming pool and the deck all around it. Let me tell you. He made a profit, but he said he was going to keep it himself. We got moved in the same trailer court as Mom and Gary's trailer, and Michele was now getting her hormones. She was going off the Richter scale. She ended up, you got it, pregnant.

On a Saturday night, we did about 320 customers in a ninety-seat restaurant. Like I said, I don't brag. I cooked over thousands of steaks, and only three ever came back. Two were underdone, and for the other one, a customer asked me for medium rare but wanted rare, not my mistake but still a wrong order, I refried the steak again, and the guy sent it back again. It was rare, and the owner was getting angry! On the third attempt, I cooked it the way I liked it, a minute on each side, and the man loved it and left a huge tip for the waitress!

On that same Saturday night, I asked a guy, whom everyone said looked like Clark Kent, if the corn were hot. At the end of the night, I asked the owner if everything were all right. Her reply was everything was okay but one order of corn.

Christmas was coming up, and I wasn't about to go there. You know what I mean, so I didn't. Judy didn't, and I didn't. Right after that altercation, I got a letter stating, if you want to live, don't come up here. And he was a damn good shot. I thought, *No problem here.*

It so happened that I don't know what you call it, but exactly forty days later, the man went blinder than a bat. It was something with the eyeballs. Freaky maybe. I don't think grasping it ole.

Oh, yeah, thanks to the Portland Trailblazers for taking Bowie over Michael because we are still winning championship basketball.

One day, Dad was thinking something evil. I said that was what he deserved. Would you believe it? Forty days later, he just lost one eye.

It was starting to get cool here on October 20, so I came in. Judy was saying some crazy stuff, things like having her hospitalized or committed. She bought us our wedding ring. Wait a minute here. There were three weddings, and I hadn't bought one wedding ring and was divorced with two. Hell, that was batting a thousand. Remember October 20, Greg birthday. That will be easy to remember.

The worst blizzard was getting ready to dump a lot of snow on us. I think Cincinnati got four inches. Where we were, it was twenty-four inches. Portsmouth got thirty-eight inches. Everywhere it snowed. It was the freakiest storm I have ever seen.

It was getting to be payday for someone. Yep, it's me. Ridicule my brother's sinus problems. I mean, bust a vessel in me. I mean, I ripped them good. But when it was my turn, forty sinuses came visiting me for the rest of my life. Amen!

The big discovery I made was how I learned what kind of talk I have. I don't remember. On Saturdays they had this one where they teach you some English. I fell in love with this one where you talk with interjections. I always speak with so much gusto. Like Pappy says, the word will never hurt you. He doesn't play the harmonica anymore, but one thing each of us can do is dance.

Chester died. I was a pallbearer for him. He got in a hurry to unload his tanker in the pouring rain. The sleeves or clamps didn't fit that well, and it sprayed all over his body. His lungs breathed in the fumes. That really did a number on him. I knew what a proud man he was. At the hospital, he would pull all the IVs in his arm, so they sent him home for the rest of his life, but Mom lived right next door to her.

When I saw Morris Bloomfield at the funeral, he said he knew that Firebird was mine with his Paul Newman grin. I asked if he were still taking titles for titles.

"Well of course," he said.

Somehow I got talked into going to her parents' house for Christmas.

Well, I thought, *he's blind now so I guess I'll be all right. But be leery and weary with one eye open always.*

Judy got hired on has a waitress at the vineyard and made good money at it. I was working in my laboratory to fix specials and noticed they hired a guy who looked like Clark Kent from Superman. He had the glasses, and to me, that was it.

Then at the Labor Day reunion, I was told that, when we were back to back, you could not tell us apart. In high school, we visited, and I was on a motorcycle with a helmet on, of course.

Some kid kept saying, "Joel, Joel, and Joel."

I said, "I'm not Joel."

I didn't understand why he would call me that, but after Judy told me she could not tell the difference unless we turned around, I didn't know if Joel, another brother, was identical or not. Things just seemed freaky. I asked Joel about Richard Fields. My dad said he was a good man and everything else. He told me that he wasn't my real dad. He took Mom to the hospital and used his last name on the birth certificate because Mom would be called gutter trash, luring them on, slut, or whore. I think you get the picture. So instead of that, he said he was the father of me, but he wasn't my real dad.

But still today in the family, all the first cousins don't know anything at all in the life and times of me. But like I said, I'm running behind time. She got me a Sega Genesis game, and it's all right, but I found a game at R-mart one day, Pebbles Beach Golf Course. I still play it today. I played five thousand games of it and shot sixteen under once and fifteen under twice for about twenty years. It's a great game. My average is about seven under a game. Beat that record.

Jordan's gone to baseball now, so I wish him all the luck in the world there. I know the NBA misses him.

Mamaw turned to worst by drinking too much saccharine pop. She started turning yellow around her body. Her heart was still as strong as ever, but her liver was serious. She was the first to die in the Eachus family. Yes, I was a pallbearer for her. She raised me in the prime of my life. It rained all day long, but on the way to work, the clouds lifted, and sunshine came out. But she died on my way there. I got a call that she passed away, and she was given morphine for pain.

I got a better job now at an Inn in town. I was lots closer to work. I was flipping eggs in the air with my trusty skillet. I met a pretty cool cat there, Larry. He looked like a pit bull to me, but he had a cousin named Brandy. She worked the first day I was there. I asked him about her.

He said, "That's my cousin, meaner than a wildcat on steroids."

She came in one night without work clothes on. She had on a pair of blue jeans, and I was wowed. I always thought Elly May Clampett had the most beautiful thighs in the world.

I asked her one day, "If you want to wear that shirt again next time …"

I didn't really think she heard me, but next day, you got it. She wore it again. Now I heard this woman beat the hell out of men for supper. Nothing happened. I had my chance, but I stayed true to my honor. I did owe her the honor. If I ever saw her, I did owe her that.

Pappy passed away the following year due to loneliness, I guess, being married for sixty years. One good thing now was that Jordan came back to the NBA. Amen!

Now I was starting to do something I never really did before, watching TV. I had a VCR so I started recording *Star Trek*, *Sactman*, and *Nimoy* series. Then there was a show called *Taxi*. Then there was the *Three Stooges*, *Beverly Hillbillies*, and finally *Married with Children*. I watched every episode. Ronnie, who introduced Dad to my mom, passed away from cancer.

On October 20, 1998, again after twenty-one and a half years, I got a phone call from Mom saying someone had stopped over to visit us. I drove on over to the two blocks away. My back was really getting worse every day. I got there and saw a one-and-a-half-year-old blonde girl in there. She was named Kelsey Dawn and had been born on July 9, 1997. With her was a blonde-headed woman, her mother-in-law, and grandma-in-law. That woman, come to find out, was my daughter, Miss Wendy Sue. I felt warmth return in me so fast that I never felt in my life. God was so good to bring her back into my life again. We talked for a while. I asked why now she told me. Granny talked her into coming, along with her mother-in-law.

Why hadn't she come sooner? She was told I was gay, and she held that against me. But that wasn't true. Her mother, of course, had deceived her. She kept her promise of making life hell for her, and she did keep her promise on that end of the deal. Now I visit her at least three times a year.

I had to start my new job as maintenance man for the Inn. The best manager to work for, Kenny Cooley, met me on the same day my daughter came back into my life. Yep, you know the date, October 20, 1998.

Ellery and I went to visit Wendy Sue one weekend. It was cold, so I wanted a cigarette bad. I went outside with a tank top, a pair of shorts, and sandals. It was about zero degrees outside. The wind chill was fifteen below. I finished my cigarette. It felt like a knife went through my lower lung area. Two weeks later, I had pneumonia. The boss took it easy on me for two weeks until I felt better. He's a great boss, like I told you.

It was the turn of the century now. 2000 didn't flare up like they said. Then in 2002, Wendy gave birth to Melody Isabella Faith Wright on February 1. Kelsey Dawn was now an older sister. Later that year, you got it. It was a Labor Day reunion for us. Mom looked worse for wear. She said her sinuses were bothering her. She went to the doctor next day, and she hated doctors her whole life.

I called her that night to check her out. She was in my old bedroom, watching something, and I told her I loved her. That was the last time I ever heard her voice. I went to work again at Moyer's Vineyard again. Before I got into the parking lot, I was told my mom was heading toward the hospital. Would you believe it? My car started sputtering bad. I just barely made it home, but Ellery's car was there. I had the extra key for it in case he locked himself out.

She bled to death. Around her lungs, it hemorrhaged blood like crazy. It was like a break in a water pipe. Blood was everywhere in the bathroom. Clumps of blood were on the counter and the sink. We found out she had TB. We all had to be tested for it. I had to take some pills forever, or it seemed like that to me.

I made the top ten news one year. On a wintry day, I was heading home to get my stash and some food for the kids. I was in an accident. Some guy was following this car in front of him. He got into my lane. I was laughing, thinking he shouldn't be driving in this weather with his big truck. Well, it kept getting closer. Then bam! The front end of his truck was going along the top of my driver side of the car. All I saw was the bottom of his truck. I got out, staggering in the snow. He had cut my car off. I first saw the driver of the truck coming my way. He asked if I were all right.

"Woozy, of course," I said. "I'm fine."

They called the ambulance. On the way there, a car was stranded on the side of the road. A man was working on his car. His mother was in the car. I worked with her at the Inn. She was a dishwasher. The ambulance struck him with its side mirror and killed him. That was the reason I made the top ten that year because they were coming to get me.

One day, I came in and told my manager, Brenda Donald, to keep her eyes on Margaret, the dishwasher. That night, she had a stroke. Now they were calling me the "Grim Reaper." I didn't want me to look at them now.

I was proud of a little girl from our region, Heather Renee French, because she won the Miss USA competition. She stood up for the Disabled American Veterans because her dad was one.

My back pains were getting severe now, all the time aching. My wife talked me into going to the VA hospital. A quarter pound of pot wasn't cutting the mustard anymore. Now it was time for the doctor.

Ellery graduated two months later. He was out driving in the really dense fog. He ran off the road and hit the only tree there. That was a good thing. Below was about a thousand-foot drop to the bottom of the valley. They had to use the jaws of life to get him out. Kenny, who retired at the Inn, helped rescue him. The fog was still really dense. No helicopter would fly from Lexington. They took an ambulance and got him there. The whole right side of his brain from back to end was purple and black. He also had a lacerated liver. He was only eighteen then. The doctors said he would be fine. He was out of it for one week before easing him off the morphine. This most purple color started walking with him. He wore Depends diapers for three months. The only thing that saved the guy with him was that he weighed about four hundred pounds. The doctors had to reset his pelvic bone twice before they got it right. He was disabled from that wreck. Ellery tried to rebound but couldn't. We were taking him to

Drake in Cincinnati one day, and some pilots ran into the World Trade Center in New York. Then veterans were recognized again.

In October 2003, my Aunt Carla died. She had just turned fifty the month before. I would be fifty tomorrow. With the love of Jesus in my sweet blue eyes, I made it to fifty. One day while I was working, I reached down to get a cooking sheet. Then bam! My back really made me wince harshly. *Old man, I think your time is up*, I thought.

I didn't want to admit it, but facts were facts. I was going to call it quits the next day, but one of the owners was like an hour late opening. I left a half hour later. I was tired of waiting. I'd been to many of these late openings.

Now I drew Social Security with my 20 percent disability from the VA. My nerves were getting the best of me. Now my youngest stepdaughter was a nightmare on Elm Street, popping kids out of her. Then the VA doctor gave me some nerve pills. I worked up to answer the phone one day. I reached for it. After that, I don't remember falling in the kitchen, just laying there. I couldn't move my right leg.

The ambulance came. I broke my tibia. It was cleanly cut at the bottom, but the top was splinted every way possible. I had to go to the VA. The next day, they saw it and the x-rays. They called a specialist, who had to put a rod from my knee to my ankle with clamps and swivels in it.

I was saved in 1975. I was a member of a church. I loved going to it until 1998, when I heard a bunch of hypocrites jamming in the back pews, doing people awful. I went for one reason, to hear the sermon from the preacher. If this book works out, I will donate 10 percent of my profits, or tithes, to the church I'm a member of. And if it's still the same, I'll just go to another church somewhere. Now I am up to date. I had shattered my tibia.

During this time, my third friend died. His name was Timmy. I was still using my crutches to get around. I went to his visitation. It didn't seem possible because I had just seen him a month earlier. I was on crutches at the time, and I was going to chew the fat with him. But his mom said something to me that got me all choked up, saying I was Timmy's best friend that he ever had. All his other so-called friends only used him for their monetary gain, but I never did.

My nerves were getting to me now, so I went to see a shrink at the VA hospital in Cincinnati to help me. I started taking some nerve medicine to calm me down.

Around this time, Wendy Sue gave birth to my youngest granddaughter, Brittney Susann Wright, on July 25, 2008. Brittney was a twin, but her twin died halfway through Wendy's pregnancy, but the Lord blessed us with Brittney, a little firecracker in appearance and temperament, just like her pappy.

I was taking it hard when my stepdaughter Gwen started having kids because I couldn't work anymore.

One day in 2008, my wife and I saw a piece of land out in the country on top of a hillside, and at the bottom of the hill was where Pappy and Mamaw lived at in Springdale, where my mom, the twin, and Satha were born. One thing about Margaret, Satha, and Mom, they never touched a drop of alcohol in their whole lives. I think it was because an alcoholic raped my mom.

We bought the land and moved a double wide on top of it, and that was my dream house, everything a man could possibly want. Some Amish family helped construct it. They built me a ramp for my electric wheelchair. My stepdaughter and two kids started going to school, and every morning at five thirty, I could hear her scream at the kids, combing their hair and pulling their hair. I took it for two years, and I just couldn't stand it anymore.

So you got it, on October 20, I left the premises. My son and I left to go to one of his friends. He was a really nice guy and everything.

One day I moved over to Greg's house because Dad had just died six months earlier. Then it finally happened. I was out of my mind and shipped to the ER. I couldn't walk, talk, or do anything but just have a stupid look on my face. That night, a storm struck our region. Everything came to a standstill. Some guy next to me was ate up with cancer. No helicopter could come out in the storm. Everything was grounded.

By the end of January, I was called the OD kid. I was rushed to the hospital five times, but the last time, I was still the same. I couldn't walk, talk, or do anything. I figured out what was causing these problems, but it was too late. The VA canceled all my pain meds and nerve pills and found out my nerve pills were causing all the trouble. They all thought it was the pain meds, the hospital where I lived and the VA too. One night my son was working, and it was so cold. With the wind chill, it was about thirty below zero.

When he got in, I told him, "Let's go get some Bacardi 151."

Earlier I had my feet inside the oven with no shoes on, trying to get them puppies warm. The house where we were staying had walls with some major cracks in them, and the wind just came right on in to freeze my ugly ass.

Like I said, I am not afraid of anything at all, but that was about to come to an end. I started hearing things that scared the hell out of me, and it was the nerve pills causing all my worries. I took the first drink I ever had in twenty-one years. I had to get out of this house I was in, so I moved next door to my dream home where my ex lived. Oh, I didn't pay for any divorce again. I was three for three, like the wedding rings. Very many people can't say that.

I lived there for about six months. Then the Housing Authority called and said they had a room for my son and me.

I was trying to get my pain meds back, but I didn't have any luck. They said I needed to go to eight south at the VA hospital for rehab for twenty-one days, so I quit smoking there. But when I was there, a really nice black woman talked to me and told me what I needed to do, but I was having a hard time to go to sleep. An assistant helped me out to support my back, and I couldn't thank her enough.

On a Friday, I fell asleep for a class, and I felt bad because I was supposed to go to every class. Then for the first time in my life, I got in place.

She replied, "Get your white ass back there and shut up."

Wow!

After twenty-one days, I was going to go home and buy me a TV and some furniture. My

ALVIN WRIGHT

son picked me up, and when I got home, I was knocked down by some of the worst news I could have. I called the bank, and they replied that I owed them almost two dollars. My jaw dropped to the floor. I just got paid a day before I got out of eight south, and sure enough I owed them about two dollars.

What happened was that I had a girl in my house getting a piece of tail. At eight south, you can't have any phones or anything like that, but it wasn't she who did it. He let a junkie heroin freak in my home, and he stole my debit card, without me so knowing it. She even slept in my bed. I told him nobody could stay here. When I was gone, so much for that. So here I was, $650 gone like the wind in the willow. I felt like I could use a cigarette, but I didn't. Amen!

So just for the equinox, out of the corner of my eye, I thought I had a vision. A quasar hit out of the blue, but that was impossible. A quasar! Get real, Alvin. Then it happened again one day. No one saw this but me, so later on I observed it again. Was I losing my mind or what? It was just a whim or something.

Then one day I saw someone was talking to this quasar. I confronted him and my son. He said about fifteen minutes later that he wasn't talking to anyone. Yep, yep, I was losing it. One of his friends, a lesbian, was talking to this vision I was seeing. She denied talking to anyone. That was it. I'd done lost it.

I didn't have that vision anymore, so it was almost equinox again on a warm March day. I was sitting outside. Then bam! There it was again, a quasar talking to some of my son's friends. I talked to him. Then he told whom he was talking to. Oh my God, I was not losing my mind after all. Man, what a relief.

One day I confronted this quasar face-to-face. She moved from Atlanta, Georgia. She had four kids and raised them all by her lonesome, asking help from nobody. Wow! Now I was the kind of person who would give the shirt off my back to help someone all my life, if he or she is willing to try. That's why I called her Quasar still today, even on my telephone. She's the nicest women you want to meet. I told her, if she ever needed anything, I could help her if I could. Amen!

At eight south, they make you answer questions. Everything I wrote was about God. Amen!

Trust me. I do not lie about anything. There wasn't any hanky panky because I am not that damn lucky. One thing I found out about life is that, man, I have the worst luck in my life of failing to ask someone as beautiful creatures. My whole life, I am zero for sixty for failing. All the women I had were introduced to me by someone. Amen! Except for Brandy. She didn't say yes, but she didn't say no.

I didn't watch TV at all, nothing but sports and *Jeopardy*. One day I was driving, listening to the Reds on the radio. Brennaman was talking about a show that he wanted to get home and watch called *Swamp People*. People, I fell in love with that show because I always wanted to tackle one of them gators my whole life.

When I was watching it, I saw a preview of *Counting Cars*. Because I love autos better than the Count, I've taken extreme pride with my vehicles my whole life. It's completely off the Richter scale.

One day I was channel surfing, and I saw a guy pull in a three hundred-pound fish. I loved to fish with the best of them. It was called *Wicked Tuna*. I would simply love latching onto one of them bad boys. Then I saw another show *Mud Cats*, where they caught them with their bare hands.

Finally after two years, they were going to put in my access ramp at my front door. Amen!

Now I am smoking the streets in my wheelchair, waving and smiling like an opossum on a hot Saturday night. One day I was strolling along the avenue when some rookie cop pulled a pit maneuver on me and scared the crap out of me. My name was on the radio bank. One minute later, Quasar called to see if I were all right. I was so stunned that I couldn't think, or I would have given them hell all over the avenue.

One day I decided to start collecting cans on the roads, and you would be surprised how many that I could find out there on the streets.

Like I've been telling you, I'm the nicest person you would want to meet, or I could be your worst nightmare you can have. My motto I got from Pappy is "Start no trouble, and there won't be no trouble." I pray every time I go out. I take no money with me, just my phone in case of emergencies. I am not going to feel sorry for the poor sap who is trying to rob me unless I'm having a good hair day, but that is very seldom.

But when I was a kid living in the big metropolis of the States, I learned two things really fast. Like Pappy said, "Start no crap" because, in the cities, they will peel your noggin for you. The main one is "Never ever go into someone's yard because that's their property, unless you are asked to."

I learned quickly that there's all kinds of people in the world, good and bad. Then one day I watched a show on TV, *Criminal Minds*, which I do not recommend for children at all, but the show is correct about a lot of things about the demented people out there. Trust me. I met a lot of them. But one show I watched when I was a kid is still on TV today, and it still makes me laugh. It's Bugs Bunny.

But one night on late-night TV, Johnny Carson was ending. His career was up. He had Clint Eastwood on there, the reason I watched it. He said *The Outlaw Josey Wells* was the best movie he ever made. He wasn't lying. I didn't see it until about a couple months ago, and I loved it. But before that, the last time I saw him make a movie I liked was *Dirty Harry*. Like I say, I hardly ever watch TV at all, except for sports.

The last thing I can think about is me. Like I say, words will never hurt you physically, but mentally, it can be a big strain on the heart. When we were moving all the time out to California, kids would really ridicule me because, like I said, I was five feet tall in the fourth grade. I heard words like freak, homily, gruesome, ugly, or any other name you could think of. I never mentioned my big noggin. I got a size eight and a quarter head, and the kids really ridiculed my big ears, like Bugs Bunny and Dumbo. I was verbally insulted. Then when I got a lot older, they quit calling names like that, until, like I said earlier, my name got changed. The guys would call me the b-word. And sorry enough, I got it from all my wives as well. So that was something I just couldn't handle. I didn't ask to be born because my mom was raped, but I wouldn't change a thing because I have two great kids, three grandkids, and two step-granddaughters.

One night right before I was going to bed, I was surfing the TV channels. For some reason, the Golf Channel had a movie on it that really shocked me, *The Legend of Bagger Vance*. When this little boy who had no fear asked this guy named Junah why he drank, he said, "To kill some brain cells." But when he said the memory cells, they were the tough sons of bitches to kill because he wasn't lying at all. No alcohol or drugs can kill them cells, and he was right. Amen!

Maybe one day I might find me some beautiful lady who will go out with me, if she can get by all the acne craters I have all over my face and back. I have some deep craters, and still today I cannot stand to look at myself in the mirror when I shave, just because of all the words they told me my whole life.

If you can help someone, do it for the sanity of the world. In concluding this story, in which there is a lot of things I forgot to mention, at least it's a start. Amen!

On July 3, 2014, my son Ellery went to some girl's house and passed out. She helped two guys lift my house key from him. They broke into my house with lights shining into my eyes and said, "Do as I say and you won't get hurt!" He had a gun and a knife, and he said to keep my hands above my head. I told him the money was in my shorts on the wheelchair. They cleaned me out. About six months later, I still have nightmares and flashbacks about that night and the lights.

October 20, 2014, rolled around, and I thought I would go back to church. I went back fifty years later in my wheelchair with my Book. I went to the side door, and I was locked out of the church. I was furious for about two seconds. I heard singing hymns, and I went to the front of the church and listened. I saw a bicycle beside the door, and the last person I would have ever thought of in the world appeared. It was Harley. It was his bike that I saw.

Harley can't talk at all, but he listens well. I guess he went back inside to try to explain but was unable to because of his handicap. But I went back home. When I got home, folks, I was crying and gully washing down my cheeks for two or three minutes. I never had before experienced the tears of joy from the Lord. The Lord is great! Now Harley and I are best friends. I asked him when his birthday was. He did not know, so I said I'd make it May 16, just like mine.

A couple weeks later, I called the bank to see how much money I had in my account. They told me $75,000, and my jaw dropped. The VA finally came through. Praise the Lord again!

In 2015, I was sick and tired of passing people up, and they sped up on me to make it harder for anyone to pass them. Sick people they are. Semis did this as well. It wasn't just cars, and my poor Impala had no power for passing. I went to a car lot and saw my car, and I got my dream car, a 2013 Dodge Challenger with silver exterior and charcoal inside. I must say this car is sharp! A head turner too! Boy, can it go!

I went to church again, and the door was unlocked. This time they said they had been having break-ins lately. I gave more to the church in donations like I always do, and it makes the Lord happy.

I asked my brother Gary if he wanted to take a trip with me to Vegas in my new car. Of course, he said yes. I told him why. Wendy had saved my Murray pedal car from the junk heap in 2004. She had kept it for me for years. She had seen a show on the History Channel called *Rick's Restorations*. I paid for the gas, and he paid for the rooms on our way out to Vegas. Gary and I went out to Wendy Sue's home and got the fire truck without her knowing about it. Anthony, my son-in-law, did know.

On the way to Vegas, I asked Gary what was the fastest he had ever reached in a car. He replied 125 miles per hour. Well, my car went over 140 miles per hour in Wyoming. It was nighttime coming into Vegas. Remember in 1963, I said it looked like a 49ers camp, but now there was no end to the lights in Vegas! Oh my goodness, I could not believe how huge this city had gotten!

While there, we went to a lot of other places, and brother, it was hot there in June 2015. The coolest temperature was a hundred degrees at six o'clock in the morning. My brother and I had a wonderful time while there. I don't gamble because I believe the Lord would strike me down, and neither did Gary. So you can still go to Vegas and have a wonderful time. Now my preacher today is thinking about going to take in the sights like we did.

It's been thirty-four years since I've had any acid because I don't have any chemists, and the only drugs I didn't like were PCP or angel dust. I had them in 1974. I sat there for hours without taking a sip out of my beer and, of course, nerve pills.

In 2016, I finally got my fire truck back from Vegas. My brother Gary helped me uncrate it since he went to Vegas with me. That's just the kind of man I am. He deserved the honor as well because that's just the way I am. And let me tell you. They knocked it out of the ballpark. I took it and surprised Wendy Sue with it, and her jaw went to the floor!

So for the ending, I hope the Lord and I can help people throughout the world by seeing all the suffering that others have caused me during my lifetime.

And finally, the two songs that sums me up are, "Lean on me. And just keep on smiling. No matter how bad it is, just keep on smiling!" In conclusion, always give your heart into the Lord for any situation for which you are in. Also the things that make me smile are the Word of the Lord, a child's laughter, turning the ignition key to hear my car start, and serving hot food to a hungry person.

There's somethings I forgot. In 1984, I told Pappy my favorite show was back on, *Jeopardy*. He watched it every day until he died in 1996. Then my daughter came back to me on, you guessed it, October 20, 1998.

One of my happiest days I had was in the winter of 1966. Some kid had a Saint Bernard. If I picked up the football, he would knock me down. I played so long that my finger and toes were frostbitten.

I've been called the Grim Reaper, Prophet, Great One, and Freak, but I'm the best person that anyone would like to like. Gary told me I was a perfectionist when I was in high school. Later Greg gave me the title of "Butcher of the English Language." You probably have the hang of it by now.

I really could predict things when I was in the navy. One thing about the Eachus house, the night I was made, they said my dad never drank again. Mom and Margaret never took a drop. Marvin, Edward Jr., Charles, and Joel were social drinkers. Carla couldn't ever get enough.

One day Marvin Jr., Carla, and her husband Pat were drinking a little. Junior went to the restroom. Carla started one of her famous drunk cries. Marvin had no mercy since he shanked his fourth-grade teacher with a pencil, which was his last day for school. Junior came back in and saw her crying. Next thing there was going to be a clash of the Titans.

Marvin said, "Junior, I'll cut your gizzard out."

Then Carla got in between them and said, "I was just kidding."

Then after that, neither one drank another drink again. Just Carla drank, and anything she said was usually a big fat lie.

If this book works out, I am going places. I've seen great people with the aura on TV, and I'll spread the word around the United States.

Three things make me smile like an opossum: the Lord, family, and kids. And when you turn the ignition switch over, it starts right up. Varoom!

I know I don't have too much time left. Like I said, I just know things like that. It's a gift from the Almighty. I just want to help out my community and the church I've gone to since 1962. I've smoked pot for pain for years until it got too bad in 2001.

In Chicago in 1965, I had no idea the Cubs had a spell on them. Then the Bulls got them a team that year or next, and I got to see their first game ever on WGN. Of course there were the Blackhawks. But if there weren't sports on TV and soaps, there would be no TV back then.

Like the hymn says, he walks with me, and he talks to me. He told me to get help writing the words from you all. My last wife is always in awe from the things I told her. I'll feel like I will be assassinated for spreading the word like our Savior. If it's good enough for him, it's good enough for me. Amen!

In the early sixties, I had the honor of seeing a guy who won the grand slam in tennis, Rod Laver. It was fantastic to watch him play, and no one has even done it again. Also I watched West Texas upset undefeated Kentucky.

The best person I ever heard was the great Paul Harvey. The things he would talk about were fantastic. There's also words from the Lord Almighty and the great Cawood Leveret for Kentucky.

One of the greatest basketball players I saw was Maurice Lexus, who won a championship at Marquette in NCAA basketball. Next year he won the championship at the Kentucky Colonels of the ABA. Then the league folded up, so he went the following year to the Portland Trailblazers and won the NBA championship. He's also known as the Enforcer!

In NASCAR, it was Buddy Baker, but you heard all the time about Richard Petty. And in golf, one who had an aura around his head and died so young was Payne Stewart with his knee-high pants he wore.

We came in from Virginia one weekend. Chester took me a ride on his motorcycle. I had a helmet on. Some kid kept on calling me Joel, my uncle.

I said, "I'm not Joel."

I took off my helmet, and he shut up then. One Labor Day reunion, we were shooting some hoops. My wife Judy said to me that Joel and I were identical twins until we turned around. It was like day and night. Joel lost his twin at birth.

But for fishing, bait filets of bluegill. It's a dinner bell for blue channel catfish. And hang on to your rods!

When Mom died in 2002, about two hundred kids she brought up into the world came to her funeral. For all the good times, they had her supervision.

On Saturday, cartoons had music for English. I found out I like to talk interjections with a one-word sentence. Also I learned in LA that instigators don't get caught. The retaliator does. That doesn't mean anything to me.

In some of my last days I got, I ride around on my wheelchair, picking up pop cans for the city on the roads. They should pay me for it. I'm kidding.

One of last things I must do is take my infection to keep my boils down a lot. Without them, I'm just one big puss bucket. I went two weeks one time like that, and I had massive boils on the back of my head. I popped that sucker seven times. I've been taking them for six years. Again, thanks, everyone, for today's technology.

I would rather lose my sight over my Bugs Bunny ears. I can hear a gnat scratch its ass one hundred yards away back then.

Just one person would make me have a lark in a birdbath to help someone out or vice versa. So help me out as how much you can, please.

Ignore bullies if you can. Where we are at, the school bus has two adults on board. I told my wife Judy that I was surprised how long it took for someone to get off, like in Colorado in the early nineties, I think.

Now this subject I'm about to talk about has been around eons ago and has come in many forms of prejudice. I have seen deacons in church walk away from me with their tails wagging between their legs. And it all comes down to how they are raised. Enough said.

Now finally me, if I brag one time, God would strike me down. All the drugs I did in this life was just for pain and nothing else. Mom always said I was the greatest listener she ever met in her life, and many other people said the same thing because it stays between the Lord, them, and me. It's priceless. But last of the thing I want to do is feel up the pews at Calvary Baptist, and with the help of the Lord and you all, I just might make it.

So it's time for me to spread my wings and take off and be a Sunday school teacher at the Calvary Baptist church where I had my life take a dramatic change. Like Pappy said, "Advice is for giving or taking." I'm doing this for our Savior. He died for us. Well, I can do the same.

Last of my thoughts is to the Lord and Savior for guiding me through all the automobile wrecks and fighting all my enemies at school. And the bullies did not gang up on me and kill me. I am giving this last word a shot. I'm the most enthusiastic person to ever walk this earth. Maybe this October 20, the Cubs might make it to the World Series with the Lord's help after seventy-seven years of sorrow.

My advice is to all the people, owners, and managers. Compliment your people. I always did, and it will go a long way to show your employees appreciation in and out of the workplace.

I also do not believe in curses. For example, the Cubs never won the World Series because they did. With the Lord's help, I saw auras on people, mostly the dead persons. I also saw auras on the survivors. I would love to go visit them because it would be an honor.

Alvin Wright
The Freak!

Printed in the United States
By Bookmasters